Surviving in KOREAN

한국어로
살아남기

Surviving in Korean
한국어로 살아남기

Samyoung Publishing House
#469-9 1F Dapsimni 3-dong, Dongdaemun-gu,
Seoul, KOREA 130-804

Authors : Yeong-Ju Lim, Sun-Shil Ahn(Sunny Ahn)
Publisher : Jeong-Rye Jeong
Publishing : Sam Young Seo Gwan
Design : Design Clip

Send all inquires to :
Tel : (02) 2242-3668
Fax : (02) 2242-3669
E-mail : sysk@paran.com
Homepage : http://www.sysk.kr

ISBN 978-89-7318-315-9 13710

price: 13,000 Won

Printed in Korea

Surviving in KOREAN

한국어로
살아남기

for
beginners

Useful Korean Language
for Learners of Korean

Samyoung Publishing House

PREFACE

Dear Readers,

We are glad to have this opportunity to invite you to the world of Korean language. Beginning a foreign language is not an easy job, but We are sure that you are already half-way to achieving it.

The book is intended to help readers not only learn basics of Korean language but acquire real-world communication skills for everyday life in Korea. And we are expecting readers to more fully understand Korea and its culture, society, and life alike by learning the language.

It was a tough job to determine how to write Korean sounds in the Roman alphabet. A Korean expression which means 'with a book', for example, can be written as either chaegeuro or chaek-eu-ro. Finally, we decided to write the sounds in the alphabet such that it describes the sounds as more closely to the standard Korean as possible.

'Naui chaek' meaning our book, for instance, is written with the punctuation mark '-' between words (or before postposition), such as na-ui; otherwise someone may mistakenly read it as na-u-i. In other words, the hyphen mark is inserted in order not to confuse readers.

Writing this textbook has given us an exciting opportunity to realize that Korean language is scientific and systematic, and we were motivated to think seriously about how to communicate correctly in Korean.

We have always had in mind that foreigners must face language barriers and obstacles while learning Korean as Korean people do the same, so we tried to explain the contents as easily and learner-friendly as we can.

Learning a foreign language is not made possible in isolation; it requires cultural understanding as well. It is meaningless to merely memorize words and grammar. Hence, the book introduces as many stories on Korean tradition, holidays, and cuisine as possible. We expect the readers to learn Korean language through cultural understanding and Korean culture through language learning.

We truly wish you great success in acquiring Korean language. And we hope that you become more interested in and knowledgeable about Korea.

Lastly, we thank Samyoungseogwan for the book to be made possible, and especially director Lee, Jang-Hee for his dedication. We appreciate their contributions to this book.

December 2008

Author 임영주, 써니 안

독자 여러분!

한국어의 세계에 들어오심을 환영합니다.

새로운 언어를 익힌다는 것이 쉽지 않음에도 한극어의 세계에 들어 온 것만으로도 당신들은 절반의 성공을 하였다고 생각합니다.

이 책이 기초적인 한국어 익히기는 물론, 한국에서의 일상 생활을 하는데 많은 도움을 주기를 바랍니다. 그리고 한국어를 통하여 한국을 이해하고 사랑하는 계기가 되었으면 합니다.

로마자 표기에서 많은 고심을 해야 했습니다. 예를 들면 '책으로'를 chaegeuro로 할 것인가, chaek- eu-ro로 할 것인가 등이 그것입니다. 여러번 생각한 끝에 한글 표준어 발음에 유의하여 로마자 표기를 했음을 밝혀둡니다.

'나의 책 naui chaek' 같은 경우에는 '-'를 넣어 표기(na-ui)하였습니다. '나우이'로 읽힐 수 있기 때문입니다. 이렇게 발음 상 혼란을 주는 경우에 로마자에 '-'를 넣었습니다.

집필하는 내내 우리 한글의 섬세함과 바로 쓰기에 대하여 많이 생각하는 계기가 되었습니다. 외국인의 입장에서 볼 때 얼마나 안간힘을 다하여 우리말과 글을 배울 것인가. 우리가 외국어에 전심전력했음에도 제대로 성과를 올리기 어려웠듯 그들도 많은 시간과 노력을 해야 한다는 것을 절실하게 공감했습니다.

그러한 고민을 알기에 좀 더 쉽게 접근하도록 친절하려고 노력하였습니다.

언어는 문화와 그 맥을 같이 합니다. 한 나라의 언어를 배우는 데 단순한 언어 익히기는 이제 의미가 없습니다. 그러므로 이 책에서는 한국의 전통과 문화재, 명절, 음식 등도 다루었습니다. 언어를 배우며 문화를 익히고 문화를 통하여 언어를 익힐 수 있다면 일거양득이 될 것입니다.

성공적인 한국어 학습을 기원합니다. 아울러 한국어를 배우면서 한국을 이해하고 사랑하게 된다면 더욱 좋겠다는 바람을 다시 한 번 가져봅니다.

출판의 제반 어려움에도 불구하고 기꺼이 출판을 결정한 삼영서관에 감사드리며, 특히 이장희 실장님께서 많이 애를 써 주셨습니다. 정말 감사드립니다.

2008. 12. 임영주, 써니 안

목차

chapter 3 Knowledge to Korean
_ 한국어 알기 [hangugeo algi]

chapter 4 Crawling to Korean
_ 한국어로 기어가기 [hangugeoro gi-eogagi]

chapter 5 Walking with Korean
_ 한국어로 걸음마 [hangugeoro georeumma]

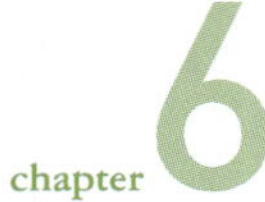

chapter 6 Taking a walk with Korean
_ 한국어로 산책하기 [hangugeoro sanchaekagi]

한국어 엿보기

hangugeo yeoppogi

01

한글 자음

hangeul ja-eum

Letter	Name	Roman	Pronun-ciation		Writing Practice		
ㄱ	기역	giyeok	g, k	**g**ang	가을 가슴	**g**a-eul / autumn **g**aseum / chest	
ㄴ	니은	ni-eun	n	**n**urse	나 나무	**n**a / I **n**amu / tree	
ㄷ	디귿	digeut	d, t	**d**oll	다리 당나귀	**d**ari / bridge **d**angnagwi / donkey	
ㄹ	리을	ri-eul	r, l	**r**ibbon	리본 라디오	**r**ibbon / ribbon **r**adio / radio	
ㅁ	미음	mi-eum	m	**m**itten	무 무지개	**m**u / raddish **m**ujigae / rainbow	
ㅂ	비읍	bi-eup	b, p	**b**ear	바다 부르다	**b**ada / sea **b**ureuda / call out	
ㅅ	시옷	siot	s	**s**it	수영 사자	**s**uyeong / swim **s**aja / lion	
ㅇ	이응	i-eung	ng / ø	E**ng**lish	응 음식	**eong** / yes **eu**msik / food	
ㅈ	지읒	ji-eut	j	**j**et	자전거 자동차	**j**ajeongeo / bicycle **j**adongcha / car	
ㅊ	치읓	chi-eut	ch	**ch**ocolate	초 차	**ch**o / candle **ch**a / tea	
ㅋ	키읔	ki-euk	k	**k**itten	케이크 크레파스	**k**eikeu / cake **k**eurepas / crayon	
ㅌ	티읕	ti-eut	t	**t**iger	타이어 타조	**t**a-i-eo / tire **t**ajo / ostrich	
ㅍ	피읖	pi-eup	p	**p**iano	포도 표범	**p**odo / grapes **p**yobeom / leopard	

Letter	Name	Roman	Pronun-ciation		Writing Practice	
ㅎ	히읗	hi-eut	**h**	horse	호랑이 해	**h**orangi / tiger **h**ae / sun
ㄲ	쌍기역	ssanggiyeok	**kk**	hi**cc**up	끄다 꿀	**kk**euda / turn off **kk**ul / honey
ㄸ	쌍디귿	ssangdigeut	**tt**	thanks	떡 딸	**tt**eok / rice cake **tt**al / daughter
ㅃ	쌍비읍	ssangbieup	**pp**	bye	뽀뽀 뿔	**pp**oppo / kiss **pp**ul / horn
ㅆ	쌍시옷	ssangsiot	**ss**	ki**ss**	쌀 싸다	**ss**al / rice **ss**ada / cheap
ㅉ	쌍지읒	ssangji-eut	**jj**		짜다 찌다	**jj**ada / squeeze **jj**ida / steam

* This Roman Symbolization has been notated based on the name of the act since July 7th 2000.
본 로마자 표기법은 2000년 7월 7일부터 시행된 것을 바탕으로 표기하였음.
Bon Romaja pyogippeobeun 2000nyeon7wol7ilbuteo sihaengdoen geoseul batangeuro pyogihayeosseum.

한글 모음

hangeul mo-eum

Letter	Letter Name	Roman symbolization		Writing Practice		
ㅏ	아	a	father	바지 사과	b**a**ji / trousers / pants s**a**gwa / apples
ㅑ	야	**ya**	**ya**rd	야구 야자수	**ya**gu / baseball **ya**jasu / palmtree
ㅓ	어	eo	lucky	어머니 어린이	**eo**moni / mother / mom **eo**rini / child
ㅕ	여	yeo	y**u**mmy	여자 여왕	**yeo**ja / woman **yeo**wang / queen
ㅗ	오	o	**o**h	오이 오징어	**o**i / cucumber **o**jingeo / squid
ㅛ	요	yo	sh**o**w	요술 요요	**yo**sul / magic **yo**yo / yoyo
ㅜ	우	u	h**ou**se	우산 우유	**u**san / umbrella **u**yu / milk
ㅠ	유	**yu**	**you**	유치원 유방	**yu**chiwon / kindergarten **yu**bang / breast
ㅡ	으	eu	tr**u**ck	그림 스케이트	g**eu**rim / picture s**eu**keite / skate
ㅣ	이	i	s**i**lver	치약 기린	ch**i**yak / toothpaste g**i**rin / giraffe
ㅐ	애	ae	**a**pple	개 대나무	g**ae** / dog d**ae**namu / bamboo
ㅒ	얘	yae	t**i**ger	얘들아 걔	**yae**deura / guys / kids g**yae** / that person
ㅔ	에	e	**e**gg	~에 게	~**e** / at, in, on g**e** / crab

Letter	Letter Name	Roman symbolization		Writing Practice	
ㅖ	예	ye	yes	예 폐	**ye** / yes p**ye** / lung
ㅘ	와	wa	w**a**ffle	~와 과일	~**wa** / and g**wa**il / fruit
ㅙ	왜	wae	w**ha**le	왜? 돼지	**wae**? / why? d**wae**ji / pig
ㅚ	외	oe	w**a**ve	외로움 괴로움	**oe**roum / loneless g**oe**roum / agony
ㅝ	워	wo	w**a**ter	원(돈) 원고지	**wo**n(don) / money **wo**ngoji / grid pad
ㅞ	웨	we	w**ai**ter	웨딩 웨이터	**we**ding / wedding **we**iteo / waiter
ㅟ	위	wi	**we**	위 위	**wi** / upper **wi** / stomach
ㅢ	의	ui		의자 의사	**ui**ja / chair **ui**sa / doctor

글자 만들기
geuljja mandeulgi

You can make up the letters by the combining of these consonants and vowels from the chart below.

다음의 자음과 모음을 결합하여 글자를 만들 수 있습니다.

[da-eumui ja-eumgwa mo-eumeul gyeorapayeo geuljjareul mandeul su isseumnida]

		ㅏ a	ㅓ eo	ㅗ o	ㅜ u	ㅡ eu	ㅣ i
ㄱ	k, g	가 ga	거 geo	고 go	구 gu	그 geu	기 gi
ㄴ	n	나 na	너 neo	노 no	누 nu	느 neu	니 ni
ㄷ	d	다 da	더 deo	도 do	두 du	드 deu	디 di
ㄹ	l, r	라 ra	러 reo	로 ro	루 ru	르 reu	리 ri
ㅁ	m	마 ma	머 meo	모 no	무 mu	므 meu	미 mi
ㅂ	b, p	바 ba	버 beo	보 bo	부 bu	브 beu	비 bi
ㅅ	s	사 sa	서 seo	소 so	수 su	스 seu	시 si
ㅇ	o	아 a	어 eo	오 o	우 u	으 eu	이 i
ㅈ	j	자 ja	저 jeo	조 jo	주 ju	즈 jeu	지 ji
ㅊ	ch	차 cha	처 cheo	초 co	추 chu	츠 cheu	치 chi
ㅋ	k	카 ka	커 keo	코 ko	쿠 ku	크 keu	키 ki
ㅌ	t	타 ta	터 teo	토 to	투 tu	트 teu	티 ti
ㅍ	p	파 pa	퍼 peo	포 po	푸 pu	프 peu	피 pi
ㅎ	h	하 ha	허 heo	호 ho	후 hu	흐 heu	히 hi

Tasting to Korean

한국어 맛보기 02

hangugeo mappogi

숫자
sutjja

Arabian number	English	Roman		Korean	
0	Zero	yeong	yeong	영	영
1	One	il	hana	일	하나
2	Two	i	dul	이	둘
3	Three	sam	set	삼	셋
4	Four	sa	net	사	넷
5	Five	o	da seot	오	다섯
6	Six	yuk	yeo seot	육	여섯
7	Seven	chil	il gop	칠	일곱
8	Eight	pal	yeo deol	팔	여덟
9	Nine	gu	a hop	구	아홉
10	Ten	sip	yeol	십	열
11	Eleven	sip il(sibil)	yeol hana	십일	열하나
12	Twelve	sip i (sibi)	yeol dul	십이	열둘
13	Thirteen	sip sam	yeol set	십삼	열셋
14	Fourteen	sip sa	yeol net	십사	열넷
15	Fifteen	sip o(sibo)	yeol da seot	십오	열다섯

Arabian number	English	Roman		Korean	
16	Sixteen	sip yuk(simnyuk)	yeol yeo seot	십육	열여섯
17	Seventeen	sip chil	yeol il gop	십칠	열일곱
18	Eighteen	sip pal	yeol yeo deol	십팔	열여덟
19	Nineteen	sip gu	yeol a hop	십구	열아홉
20	Twenty	i sip	seu mul	이십	스물
21	Twenty one	i sip il (isibil)	seu mul hana	이십 일	스물하나
22	Twenty two	i sip i (isibi)	seu mul dul	이십 이	스물둘
30	Thirty	sam sip	seo reun	삼십	서른
40	Forty	sa sip	ma heun	사십	마흔
50	Fifty	o sip	swin	오십	쉰
60	Sixty	yuk sip	ye sun	육십	예순
70	Seventy	chil sip	il heun	칠십	일흔
80	Eighty	pal sip	yeo deun	팔십	여든
90	Ninty	gu sip	a heun	구십	아흔
100	One hundred	baek	baek	백	백

시간

sigan

Time	Roman	Korean	
One o'clock	han si	한 시	1시
Two o'clock	du si	두 시	2시
Three o'clock	se si	세 시	3시
Four o'clock	ne si	네 시	4시
Five o'clock	daseot si	다섯 시	5시
Six o'clock	yeoseot si	여섯 시	6시
Seven o'clock	ilgop si	일곱 시	7시
Eight o'clock	yeodeol si	여덟 시	8시
Nine o'clock	ahop si	아홉 시	9시
Ten o'clock	yeol si	열 시	10시
Eleven o'clock	yeolhan si	열한 시	11시
Twelve o'clock	yeoldu si	열두 시	12시

요일

yoil

Days of the week	Roman	Korean
Sunday	iryoil	일요일
Monday	woryoil	월요일
Tuesday	hwayoil	화요일
Wednesday	suyoil	수요일
Thursday	mogyoil	목요일
Friday	geumyoil	금요일
Saturday	toyoil	토요일

일요일	월요일	화요일	수요일	목요일	금요일	토요일
Sunday	Monday	Tuesday	Wednesday	Thursday	Friday	Saturday

날짜

naljja

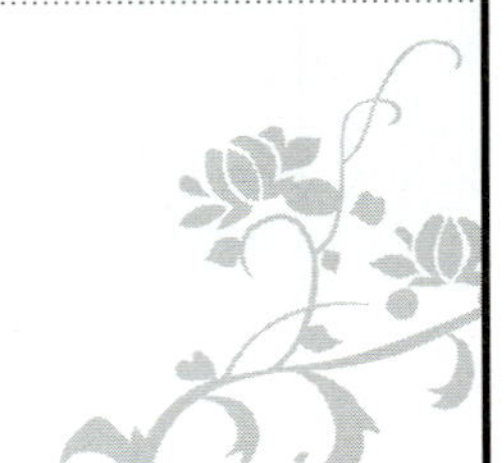

Number	English	Roman	Koean
1	1st	i ril	일 일
2	2nd	i il	이 일
3	3rd	sam il	삼 일
4	4th	sa il	사 일
5	5th	o il	오 일
6	6th	yuk il (yugil)	육 일
7	7th	chil il (chiril)	칠 일
8	8th	pal il (paril)	팔 일
9	9th	gu il	구 일
10	10th	sip il (sibil)	십 일
11	11th	sip iril (sibiril)	십 일 일
12	12th	sip i il (sibi-il)	십 이 일
13	13th	sip sam il	십 삼 일
14	14th	sip sa il	십 사 일
15	15th	sip o il (siboil)	십 오 일
16	16th	sip yuk il (simnyugil)	십 육 일
17	17th	sip chiril	십 칠 일
18	18th	sip pal il (siparil)	십 팔 일
19	19th	sip gu il	십 구 일
20	20th	i sip il (isibil)	이 십 일
21	21st	i sip iril (isibiril)	이 십 일 일
22	22nd	i sip i il (isibi-il)	이 십 이 일
23	23rd	i sip sam il	이 십 삼 일
24	24th	i sip sa il	이 십 사 일

Arabic	English	Roman	Koean
25	25th	i sip o il (isiboil)	이십오일
26	26th	i sip yuk il (isimnyugil)	이십육일
27	27th	i sip chiril	이십칠일
28	28th	i sip paril	이십팔일
29	29th	i sip gu il	이십구일
30	30th	sam sip il (samsibil)	삼십일
31	31st	sam sip-iril (samsibiril)	삼십일일

Months •

달(월)

dal(wol)

Month	Arabian	Roman	Korean
January	1	il wol (irwol)	일 월
February	2	i wol	이 월
March	3	sam wol	삼 월
April	4	sa wol	사 월
May	5	o wol	오 월
June	6	yu wol	유 월
July	7	chil wol (chirwol)	칠 월
August	8	pal wol (parwol)	팔 월
September	9	gu wol	구 월
October	10	si wol	시 월
November	11	sip il wol(sibirwol)	십 일 월
December	12	sip i wol (sibiwol)	십 이 월

단위

danwi

English	Roman	Korean	Practice
People	myeong	명	Three children 아이 세 명 [ai se myeong]
	bun	분	Two adults 어른 두 분 [eoreun du bun]
	saram	사람	One person 한 사람 [han saram]
Thing	gae	개	One apple 사과 한 개 [sagwa han gae]
	mari	마리	Four dogs 개 네 마리 [gae ne mari]
	geuru	그루	Two trees 나무 두 그루 [namu du geuru]
	jang	장	Two towels 수건 두 장 [sugeon du jang]
	jan	잔	One cup of coffee 커피 한 잔 [keopi han jan]
	dae	대	One car 자동차 한 대 [jadongcha han dae]

[Two adults 어른 두 분]

[Four dogs 개 네 마리]

Moment •

때

ttae

English	Roman	Korean
This year	ol hae(orae)	올 해
Last year	jinan hae	지난 해
Next year	da-eum hae	다음 해
This month	ibeon dal	이번 달
Last month	jinan dal	지난 달
Next month	da-eum dal	다음 달
This week	ibeon ju	이번 주
Last week	jinan ju	지난 주
Next week	da-eum ju	다음 주
Weekend	jumal	주말
Weekdays	jujung	주중
The day before yesterday	geujeokke	그저께
Yesterday	eoje	어제
Today	oneul	오늘
Tomorrow	nae-il	내일
The day after tomorrow	nae-il more	내일 모레
Morning	achim	아침
Noon	jeong-o	정오
Afternoon	ohu	오후
Evening	jeonyeok	저녁
Night	bam	밤
Midnight	jajeong	자정
Late night	neujeun bam	늦은 밤
This morning	oneul achim	오늘 아침

English	Roman	Korean
Tomorrow morning	nae-il achim	내일 아침
Tomorrow afternoon	nae-il ohu	내일 오후
Tomorrow evening	nae-il jeonyeok	내일 저녁
Everyday	mae-il	매일

나이

na-i

The 'age' usually stands for 'na-i' and 'yeonsei' for the elder people.
'나이' 는 보통 '나이' 라고 하며 어른들께는 '연세' 라고 합니다.

Number	English	Roman	Korean
1	1 year old	han sal	한 살
2	2 year old	du sal	두 살
3	3 year old	se sal	세 살
4	4 year old	ne sal	네 살
5	5 year old	daseot sal	다섯 살
6	6 year old	yeoseot sal	여섯 살
7	7 year old	ilgob sal	일곱 살
8	8 year old	yeodeol sal	여덟 살
9	9 year old	ahop sal	아홉 살
10	10 year old	yeol sal	열살
11	11 year old	yeol han sal	열한 살
12	12 year old	yeol du sal	열두 살
13	13 year old	yeol se sal	열세 살
14	14 year old	yeol ne sal	열네 살
15	15 year old	yeol daseot sal	열다섯 살
16	16 year old	yeol yeoseot sal	열여섯 살
17	17 year old	yeol ilgop sal	열일곱 살
18	18 year old	yeol yeodeol sal	열여덟 살
19	19 year old	yeol ahop sal	열아홉 살
20	20 year old	seumu sal	스무 살

Number	English	Roman	Korean
30	30 year old	seoreun sal	서른 살
40	40 year old	maheun sal	마흔 살
50	50 year old	swin sal	쉰 살
60	60 year old	yesun sal	예순 살
70	70 year old	ilhuen sal (ireun sal)	일흔 살
80	80 year old	yeodeun sal	여든 살
90	90 year old	aheun sal	아흔 살
100	100 year old	baek sal	백 살

The Korean Currency •

한국 돈

hanguk don

Korean Currency includes coins, paper bills and public checks.

한국 돈에는 동전, 지폐, 수표가 있습니다.

English / Roman		Arabic	Korean
conis	sip won (sibwon)	10	십 원
	osip won (osibwon)	50	오십 원
	baek won (baegwon)	100	백 원
	obaek won (obaegwon)	500	오백 원
paper bills	choen won	1,000	천 원
	ochoen won	5,000	오천 원
	man won	10,000	만 원
check	sip man won (simman won)	100,000	십만 원

Direction & Preposition •

방향과 전치사
banghyang-gwa jeonchisa

English	Roman	Korean
east	dongjjok	동쪽
west	seojjok	서쪽
south	namjjok	남쪽
north	bukjjok	북쪽
right	oreunjjok	오른쪽
left	oenjjok	왼쪽
in front of	apjjok	앞쪽
behind / at the back of	dwijjok	뒤쪽
by / side / next to	yeope	옆에
at / on the corner of	motung-ie	모퉁이에
before	jeone	전에
after	hu-e	후에
on	wi-e	위에
in	ane	안에
at	~e	~에
under	arae-e	아래에
above	wijjoge	위쪽에
the top of	kkogdaegie	꼭대기에
across from	geonneopyeone	건너편에
through	~eul tonghae	~을 통해
inside	~ane	~안에
outside	~bakke	~밖에

Various Sign •

각종 표지판

gakjjong pyojipan

English	Roman	Korean
exit	bisanggu	비상구
information	annaeso	안내소
entrance	ipkku	입구
danger	wiheom	위험
out of order	suri jung	수리 중
do not enter	churip geumji	출입 금지
non smoking	geumyeon	금연
reservation	yeyak	예약
vacancy	bi-eosseum	비었음
no parking	jucha geumji	주차 금지
handdicapped only	jang-ae-in jucha	장애인 주차
staff only	jigwonman churip	직원만 출입
restricted area	jehan guyeok	제한 구역
no honking	gyeongjeok geumji	경적 금지
tow zone	gyeonin jiyeok	견인 지역
restroom	hwajangsil	화장실
school zone	eorini bohoguyeok	어린이 보호구역
stop	meomchum	멈춤
yield	yangbo	양보
occupied	sayong jung	사용 중
pull	dangisio	당기시오
push	misio	미시오

색

saek

- **black**
  검정색
  [geomjeongsaek]

- **blue**
  파란색
  [paransaek]

- **dark blue**
  남색
  [namsaek]

- **light blue**
  하늘색
  [haneulsaek]

- **blue green**
  청록색
  [cheongnoksaek]

- **brown**
  갈색
  [galsaek]

- **dark brown**
  다갈색
  [dagalsaek]

- **light brown**
  황토색
  [hwangtosaek]

- **gold**
  금색
  [geumsaek]

- **gray(grey)**
  회색
  [hoesaek]

- **dark gray(grey)**
  진회색
  [jinhoesaek]

- **light gray(grey)**
  밝은 회색
  [balgeun hoesaek]

- **green**
  초록색
  [choroksaek]

- **dark green**
  진초록색
  [jinchoroksaek]

- **light green**
  연두색
  [yeondusaek]

- **orange**
  주황색
  [juhwangsaek]

- **pink**
  분홍색
  [bunhongsaek]

- **purple**
  보라색
  [borasaek]

- **red**
  빨간색
  [ppalgansaek]

- **tan**
  구리색
  [gurisaek]

- **white**
  하얀색
  [hayansaek]

- **silver**
  은색
  [eunsaek]

- **yellow**
  노란색
  [noransaek]

의복

uibok

- **belt**
  벨트
  [belteu]

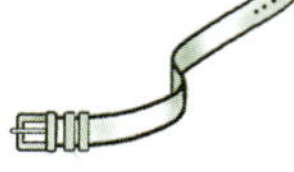

- **blouse**
  블라우스
  [bla-useu]

- **boots**
  부츠
  [bucheu]

- **coat**
  코트
  [koteu]

- **dress**
  드레스
  [deuleseu]

- **gloves**
  장갑
  [jangap]

- **cap**
  모자
  [moja]

- **jacket**
  재킷
  [jaekit]

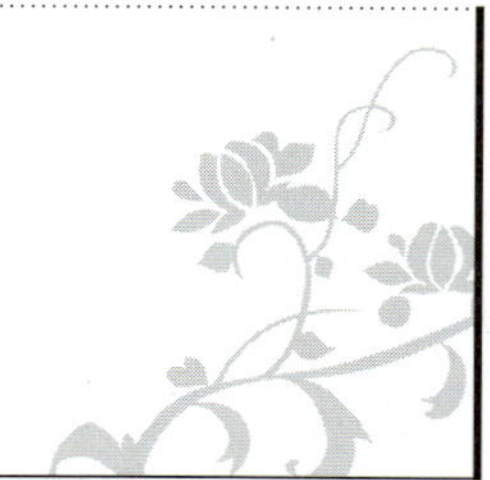

- **jeans**
  진
  [jin]

- **pants(trousers)**
  바지
  [baji]

- **sandals**
  샌들
  [saendeul]

- **shirt**
  셔츠
  [syeocheu]

- **shoes**
  슈즈
  [shujeu]

- **skirt**
  스커트 / 치마
  [seukeoteu/chima]

- **socks**
  양말
  [yangmal]

- **suit**
  정장
  [jeongjang]

- **sweater**
  스웨터
  [seuweteo]

- **tie, bow tie**
  넥타이
  [nekta-i]

- **t-shirt**
  티셔츠
  [tisyeocheu]

- **dress shirt**
  와이셔츠
  [wa-isyeocheu]

액세서리
aeksseseori

bracelet
팔찌
[paljji]

ring
반지
[banji]

key holder (=key chain)
열쇠고리
[yeolsoegori]

watch
손목시계
[sonmoksigye]

bookmark
책꽂이
[chaekkoji]

scrunches
곱창 밴드
[gobchang baendeu]

earrings
귀걸이
[gwigeori]

broach
브로치
[brojji]

necklace
목걸이
[mokgeori]

headband
머리띠
[meoritti]

신체

sinche

- **head**
  머리
  [meori]

- **hair**
  머리카락
  [meorikarak]

- **forehead**
  이마
  [ima]

- **the inner ear**
  귓속
  [gwitssok]

- **ears, ear/ears**
  귀
  [gwi]

- **occiput (=the back of the head)**
  뒤통수
  [dwitongsu]

- **ear wax**
  귀지
  [gwiji]

- **eyes**
  눈
  [nun]

- **eyelids**
  눈꺼풀
  [nunkkeopul]

- **eye brow**
  눈썹
  [nunsseop]

- **double eyelids**
  쌍꺼풀
  [ssangkkeopul]

- **eye pupils**
  눈동자
  [nundongja]

- **eyelashes**
  속눈썹
  [songnunsseop]

- **nose**
  코
  [ko]

- **runny nose**
  콧물
  [konmul]

- **whiskers**
  콧수염
  [kotssuyeom]

- **nose hole**
  콧구멍
  [kokkumeong]

- **cheek**
  볼(뺨)
  [bol(ppyam)]

● **dimple**
보조개
[bojogae]

● **mouth**
입
[ip]

● **lips**
입술
[ipssul]

● **tongue**
혀
[hyeo]

● **teeth**
이, 치아
[i, chia]

● **chin**
턱
[teok]

● **beard**
턱수염
[teokssuyeom]

● **neck**
목
[mok]

● **throat**
목구멍
[mokkumeorg]

● **shoulders**
어깨
[eokkae]

● **chest, bust**
가슴
[gaseum]

● **breast**
유방
[yubang]

● **armpit**
겨드랑이
[gyeodeurangi]

● **lungs**
폐
[pye]

● **heart**
심장
[simjang]

● **stomach**
위
[wi]

● **liver**
간
[gan]

● **kidneys**
신장
[sinjang]

● **arms**
팔
[pal]

● **hands**
손
[son]

● **wrist**
손목
[sonmok]

● **palms**
손바닥
[sonppadak]

● **fingers**
손가락
[sonkkarak]

● **finger nails**
손톱
[sontop]

- belly, stomach
  배
  [bae]

- belly button
  배꼽
  [baekkop]

- back
  등
  [deung]

- legs
  다리
  [dari]

- thigh
  허벅지
  [heobeokji]

- knees
  무릎
  [mureup]

- feet
  발
  [bal]

- ankle
  발목
  [balmok]

- toe nails
  발톱
  [baltop]

- heel(of foot)
  발뒤꿈치
  [baldwikkumchi]

- toes
  발가락
  [balkkarak]

- muscle
  근육
  [geunyuk]

- vein, artery
  핏줄
  [pitjjul]

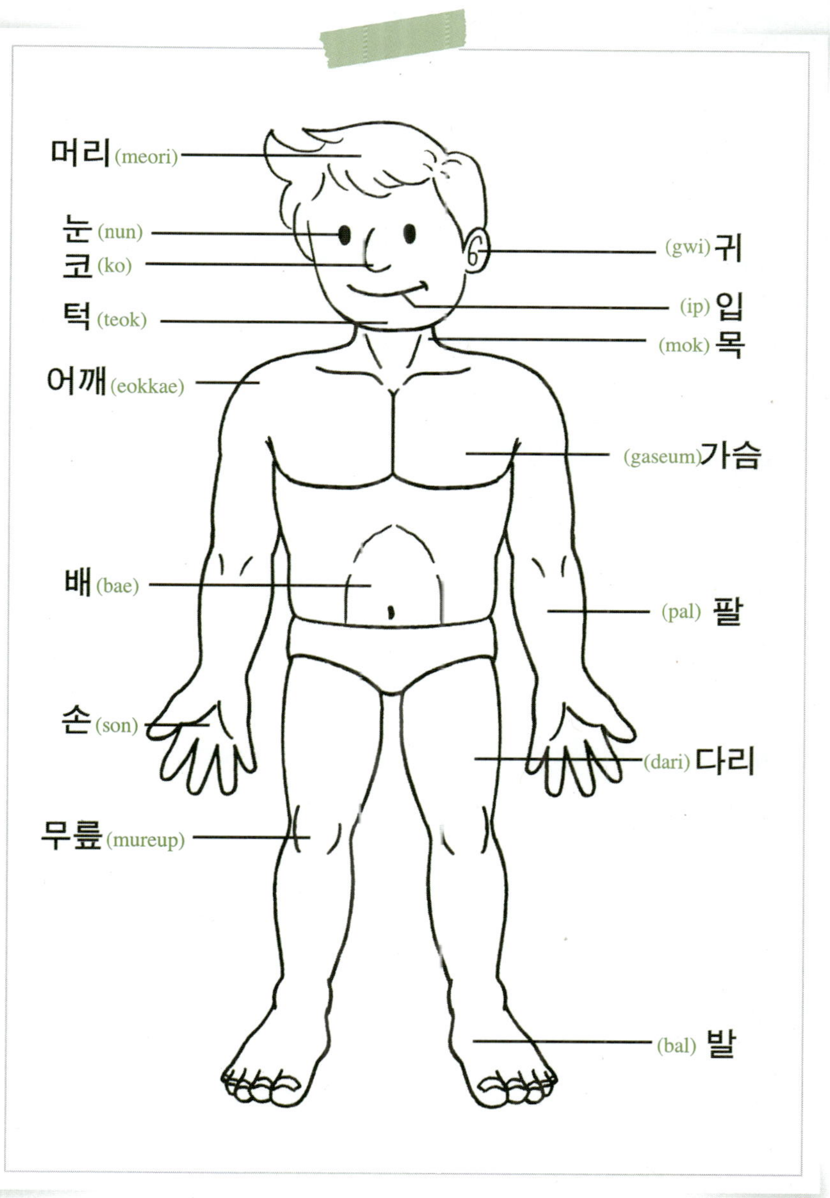

머리 (meori)
눈 (nun)
코 (ko)
턱 (teok)
어깨 (eokkae)
배 (bae)
손 (son)
무릎 (mureup)
(gwi) 귀
(ip) 입
(mok) 목
(gaseum) 가슴
(pal) 팔
(dari) 다리
(bal) 발

생활용품 / 일상용품

saenghwalyongpum / ilsangyongpum

- **washstand**
  세면대
  [semyeondae]

- **faucet/tap**
  수도꼭지
  [sudokkogjji]

- **tap water**
  수도물
  [sudonmul]

- **hot water**
  뜨거운 물
  [tteugeo-un mul]

- **cold water**
  찬물
  [chanmul]

- **toilet**
  화장실, 변기
  [whajangsil, byeongi]

- **shower head**
  샤워기
  [syawogi]

- **shower curtain**
  샤워커튼
  [syawokeoteun]

- **towel**
  타올, 수건
  [taol, sugeon]

- **towel rack**
  수건걸이
  [sugeongeori]

- **toilet paper**
  화장지, 휴지
  [whajangji, hyuji]

- **paper holder**
  휴지걸이
  [hyujigeori]

- **bath tub**
  목욕조
  [mogyokjjo]

- **bidet**
  비데
  [bide]

- **mirror**
  거울
  [geo-ul]

- **slippers**
  슬리퍼
  [seulipeo]

- **toothbrush**
  치솔
  [chissol]

- **toothpaste**
  치약
  [chiyak]

- **gargle / mouthwash**
  가글린
  [gageulrin]

- **wash the face**
  세수하다, 세안하다
  [sesuhada, seanhada]

- **soap**
  비누
  [binu]

- **shampoo**
  샴푸
  [syampu]

- **body cleanser/ body wash**
  목욕 샴푸
  [mogyok syampu]

- **conditioner**
  린스
  [rinsseu]

- **lotion**
  로션
  [rosyeon]

- **cream**
  크림
  [keurim]

- **comb**
  빗
  [bit]

- **nailclippers**
  손톱깎이
  [sontopkkakki]

- **electricity**
  전기
  [jeongi]

- **telephone**
  전화기
  [jeonhwagi]

- **television**
  텔레비전
  [telebijeon]

- **refrigerator**
  냉장고
  [naengjang-go]

- **air conditioner**
  에어컨
  [e-eokeon]

- **air purifier**
  공기 청정기
  [gonggi cheongjeonggi]

- **electric fan**
  선풍기
  [seonpunggi]

- **rice cooker**
  밥솥
  [bapsot]

- **kettle**
  주전자
  [jujeonja]

- **pot**
  냄비
  [naembi]

- **dinnerware**
  식기
  [sikki]

- **plate**
  접시
  [jeopssi]

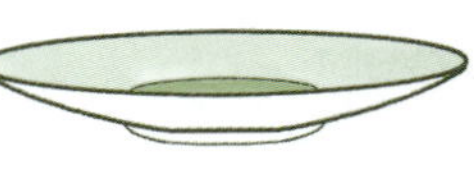

- **fork**
  포크
  [pokeu]

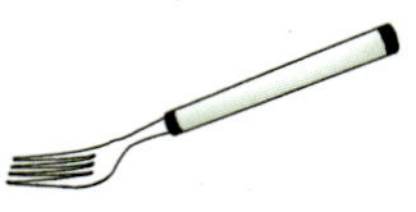

- **dining-table**
  식탁
  [siktak]

- **knife**
  칼
  [kal]

- **napkin**
  냅킨
  [naepkin]

- **tray**
  쟁반
  [jaengban]

- **spoon** 
  숟가락
  [sutkkarak]

- **chopsticks**
  젓가락
  [jeotkkarak]

- **water glass** 
  물컵
  [mulkeop]

- **coffee cup** 
  커피잔
  [keopijan]

- **ashtray**
  재떨이
  [jaetteori]

- **drawer**
  서랍
  [seorap]

- **closet**
  옷장
  [otjjang]

- **bed**
  침대
  [chimdae]

- **pillow**
  베개
  [begae]

- **blanket**
  담요
  [damnyo]

- **sheets**
  시트
  [ssiteu]

- **mattress**
  매트리스
  [maeteuriseu]

- **clock/watch** 
  시계 / 손목시계
  [sigye / sonmoksigye]

- **desk lamp** 
  스탠드
  [seutaendeu]

- **switch**
  스위치
  [seuwichi]

- **consent**
  콘센트
  [konsenteu]

- **floor**
  바닥
  [badak]

- **wallpaper**
  벽지
  [byeokjji]

- **key**
  열쇠
  [yeolssoe]

- **rag**
  손걸레
  [son-geolre]

- **mop**
  마포걸레
  [mapogeolre]

- **do laundry**
  빨래하다
  [ppalraehada]

- **broom**
  빗자루
  [bitjjaru]

- **rubber gloves**
  고무 장갑
  [gomujanggap]

- **trash bin**
  쓰레기통
  [sseuregitong]

- **scrubber**
  수세미
  [susemi]

- **disinfect**
  항균
  [hanggyun]

- **washer**
  세척기
  [secheokki]

- **vacuum cleaner**
  진공청소기
  [jingongcheongsogi]

- **laundry(=washing machine)**
  세탁기
  [setakki]

- **hand-washing**
  손빨래
  [sonppalrae]

- **laundry soap**
  액체비누
  [aekchebinu]

- **laundry basket**
  빨래통
  [ppalraetong]

- **clothesline**
  빨래줄
  [ppalraejjul]

- **laundromat**
  세탁소
  [setaksso]

- **detergent**
  세제
  [seje]

- **fabric softener**
  섬유 유연제
  [seomnyu yuyeonje]

- **bleach**
  표백제
  [pyobaekjje]

- **iron**
  다리미
  [darimi]

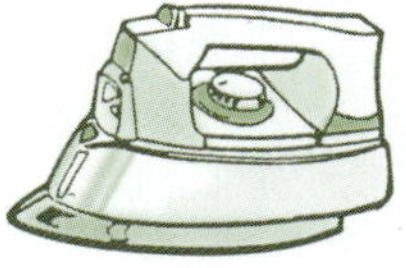

- **ironing board**
  다리미판
  [darimipan]

- **spray**
  스프레이
  [seupeurei]

- **clothes hanger**
  옷걸이
  [otkkeori]

- **dry cleaning**
  드라이
  [deura-i]

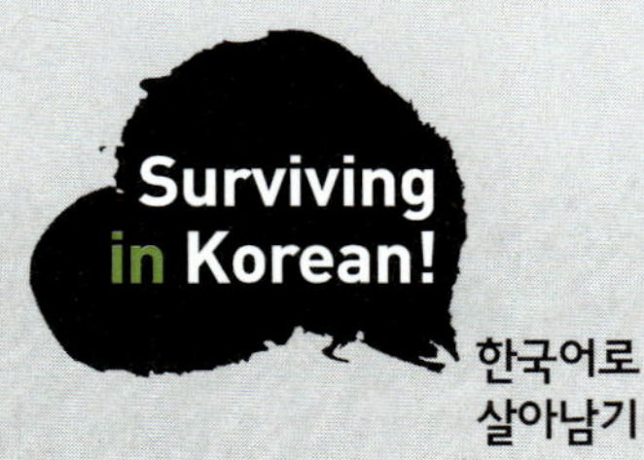
Surviving
in Korean!
한국어로
살아남기

Knowledge to Korean

한국어 알기

hangugeo algi

한국의 '도'

hangugui 'do'

The capital of Korea is Seoul, and there are 8 provinces in Korea.

한국의 수도는 서울이며 , 여덟 개 '도' 가 있다.

[hangugui sudoneun Seoul-imyeo, yeodeol gae 'do' ga itta]

English &Roman	Korean
Gyeong gi do	경기도
Gang won do	강원도
Chung cheong nam do	충청남도
Chung cheong buk do (chungcheongbuktto)	충청북도
Jeon la nam do (jeollanamdo)	전라남도
Jeon la buk do (jeollabuktto)	전라북도
Gyeong sang nam do	경상남도
Gyeong sang buk do (gyeongsangbuktto)	경상북도
Je ju do	제주도

[Province of Korea 한국의 '도']

한국의 성씨

hangugui seongssi

Korean names are made of last name and first name. And they become a full name called "seongmyeong" The names are have been noated in Roman the chart below.

한국인의 이름은 성과 이름으로 되어 있다. 이것을 '성명' 이라고 한다. 각 성씨마다 고유의 표기법이 약간씩 다르지만 로마자의 표기법에 따르면 다음과 같다.

Gan 간	Gal 갈	Gam 감	Gang 강	Gyeon 견
Gyeong 경	Gye 계	Go 고	Gong 공	Gwak 곽
Gu 구	Guk 국	Gwon 권	Geum 금	Gil 길
Gim(Kim) 김	Na(Ra) 나(라)	Namgung 남궁	Nam 남	No(Rho) 노 (로)
Do 도	Doggo 독고	Ma 마	Myeong 명	Mo 모
Mok 목	Mun 문	Min 민	Bak(Park) 박	Ban (반)
Bang 방	Bae 배	Baek 백	Beom 범	Byeon 변
Bok 복	Bong 봉	Bin 빈	Sagong 사공	Sa 사
Seo 서	Seok 석	Seonu 선우	Seol 설	Seong 성
So 소	Son 손	Song 송	Sin(Shin) 신	Sim(Shim) 심
An(Ahn) 안	Yang 양	Eo 어	Eom(Eum) 엄	Yeo 여
Yeon 연	Yeom 염	Ye 예	O(Oh) 오	Ok 옥
Wang 왕	U(Woo) 우	Won 원	Wi 위	Yu(Ryu) 유(류)
Yuk 육	Yun(Yoon) 윤	Eun 은	Eum 음	Yi(Lee, Rhee) 이(리)
In 인	Im 임	Lim 임(림)	Jang 장	Jeon 전
Jeong 정	Jegal 제갈	Je 제	Jo(Cho) 조	Ju 주
Ji 지	Jin 진	Cha 차	Chae 채	Cheon 천
Choe(Choi) 최	Chu 추	Tak 탁	Tae 태	Paeng 팽
Pyeon 편	Pyo 표	Pi 피	Ha 하	Han 한
Ham 함	Heo 허	Hyeon 현	Ho 호	Hong 홍
Hwangbo 황보	Hwang 황			

Section 03

계절
gyejeol

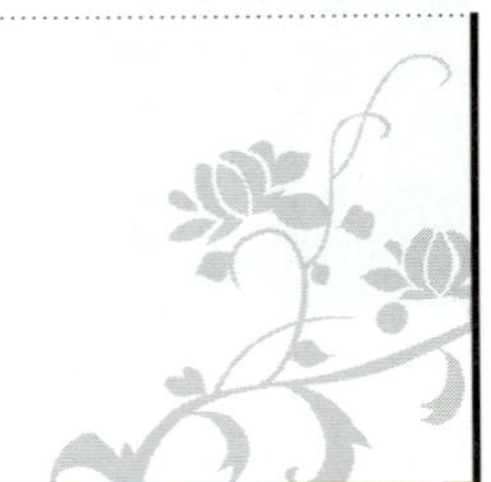

There are 4 seasons in Korea.
한국은 사계절이 있다.
[hangueun sagyejeori itta]

01 Spring | 봄   bom

- **Spring is the season between March and May.**
  보통 3월부터 5월까지를 봄이라고 합니다.
  [botong samwolbuteo owolkkajireul bomirago hamnida]

- **The spring came!**
  봄이 왔어요.
  [bomi wasseoyo]

- **It is still chilly.**
  봄 날씨가 아직 쌀쌀해요.
  [bom nalssiga ajik ssalssalhaeyo]

- **The buds bloom.**
  새싹이 났어요.
  [saessagi nasseoyo]

- **We get buds in a tree.**
  나무에 새순이 돋았어요.
  [namue saesuni dodasseoyo]

- **The cherry blossom blooms.**
  벚꽃이 피었어요.
  [beotkkochi pieosseoyo]

- **The spring wind blows.**
  봄바람이 불어요.
  [bompparami bureoyo]

- **I want to go on a picnic in the spring.**
  봄나들이 가고 싶어요.
  [bomnadri gago sipeoyo]

- **The spring rain comes.**
  봄비가 와요.
  [bombiga wayo]

- **It's getting warmer day by day.**
  날씨가 따뜻해졌어요.
  [nalssiga ttatteutae jeosseoyo]

- **There is yellow dust in spring.**
  봄에는 황사 현상이 있어요.
  [bomeneun whangsa hyeonsangi isseoyo]

● **It's really hot.**

날씨가 너무 더워요.
[nalssiga neomu deowoyo]

● **It's humid.**

날씨가 습해요.
[nalssiga seupaeyo]

● **The rainy season begins.**

장마가 시작됐어요.
[jangmaga sijak dwaesseoyo]

● **It's cool in the shade under the tree.**

나무 그늘은 시원해요.
[namu geuneureun siwonhaeyo]

● **We need to turn on the air conditioner.**

에어컨을 틀어야겠어요.
[e-eoconeul teureoya gesseoyo]

● **Summer break starts.**

여름 방학이 시작되었어요.
[yeoreum banghagi sijakdoe-eosseoyo]

● **The sun's ray is too strong.**

햇볕이 따가워요.
[haepyeochi ttagawoyo]

● **I need sun block.**

선크림이 필요해요.

[sseonkeurimi piryohaeyo]

● **Do you want to go to the beach?**
바다로 피서 갈까요?
[badaro piseo galkkayo]

● **Do you have a swimsuit?**
수영복이 있으세요?
[suyeongbogi isseuseyo]

● **The leaves turn green.**
나뭇잎이 푸르러요.
[namunnipi pureureoyo]

● **I'm thirsty.**
목이 말라요.
[mogi malrayo]

03 Autumn (Fall) | 가을

ga-eul

● **It's cool.**
날씨가 선선해요.
[nalssiga seonseonhaeyo]

● **The sky is deep and blue in the fall.**
가을 하늘은 맑아요.
[ga-eul haneureun malgayo]

● **The leaves are changing color.**
단풍이 들었어요.
[danpung-i deureosseoyo]

- **The leaves are falling.**

낙엽이 져요.

[nagyeobi jeoyo]

- **The sun's ray is too strong in the fall.**

가을 햇살이 따가워요.

[ga-eul haessari ttagawoyo]

- **It's a beautiful scene. (=) It's beautifully scenic in fall.**

가을 풍경이 아름다워요.

[ga-eul pungyeongi areumdawoyo]

- **It's a little chilly in the morning and at night.**

아침 저녁으로는 약간 쌀쌀해요.

[achim jeonyeogroneun yakkan ssalssalhaeyo]

- **The wind blows in fall.**

가을 바람이 불어요.

[ga-eul barami bureoyo]

04 | Winter | 겨울   *gyeo-ul*

- **The cold wind blows.**

찬 바람이 불어요.

[chan barami bureoyo]

- **I need a coat.**

외투를 입어야겠어요.

[oetureul ibeoya gesseoyo]

- **I need a scarf.**
  목도리가 필요해요.
  [mokttoriga piryohaeyo]

- **We need heating.**
  난방이 필요해요.
  [nanbangi piryohaeyo]

- **It's very cold.**
  매우 추워요.
  [mae-u chuwoyo]

- **My feet are freezing.**
  발이 시려워요.
  [bari siryeowoyo]

- **My hands are cold.**
  손이 시려워요.
  [soni siryeowoyo]

- **It's better to put on a pair of gloves.**
  장갑을 껴야 겠어요.
  [jangabeul kkyeoya gesseoyo]

- **The snow comes.**
  눈이 와요.
  [nuni wayo]

- **I want to go skiing.**
  스키 타러 가고 싶어요.
  [seuki tareo gago sipeoyo]

● **It's icy.**
얼음이 얼었어요.
[eoreumi eoreosseoyo]

● **The roads are slippery.**
길이 미끄러워요.
[giri mikkeureowoyo]

● **We need snow chains for the car.**
자동차에 스노우 체인이 필요해요.
[jadongcha-e seunou che-ini piryohaeyo]

한국의 명절
hangugui myeongjeol

● New Year's Day 설(설날)

: There are two different days and ways to celebrate New Years Day in Korea which are New Year's Day in Solar and Lunar year. However most of the generation prefers the Lunar new year. The New Year Day is one of the most memorable and favororble holidays in Korea. Korean people make New Year's resolution which stands for "Fortune and Luck" to their ancestors.

한국의 새해는 양력과 음력 2번 쇤다. 그러나 대부분의 기성 세대는 음력설을 선호한다. 설날은 한국 사람 최대 명절 가운데 하나이다. 새해를 맞이하여 서로 '복'을 기원하며 조상께 차례를 지낸다.

● January 1st every year

매 해 1월 1일 양력 설날
[mae hae irwol iril yangnyeok seolral]

● January 1st in Lunal calendar

음력 1월 1일, 음력 설날
[eumnyeok irwol iril, eumnyeok seolral]

● New Year's greeting 새해 인사 [saehae insa]

- 새해 복 많이 받으세요.
  [saehae bok mani badeuseyo]

● Special food on New Year's Day 설날 음식 [seolral eumsik]

- 떡국 [tteokkkuk]

- 식혜 [sik hye(sikye)]

- 수정과 [sujeong-gwa]

● Traditional play on New Year's Day 설날 놀이 [seolral nori]

– 윷놀이 [Yut nori (yunnori)]

: There are four sticks which are made of wood. You throw the sticks into the air and follow the rule by moving the marks. It's a popular board game.

나무로 만든 윷을 멍석에 던져 약속된 기호에 따라 승패를 가리는 놀이

[namuro mandeun yuseul meongseoge deonjeo yaksokdoen giho-e ttara seungpaereul garineun nori]

● Cha rye 차례 [charye]

: Prepare the traditional food for our ancestors and honor of them.

음식을 차려놓고 조상께 절을 올림. 설날과 추석에 지내는 제사를 '차례' 라고 부름

[eumsigeul charyeonoko josangkke jeoreul olrim. Seolralgwa Chuseoge jinaeneun jesareul 'Charye'rago bureum]

● Korean Thanksgiving Day 추석 [chuseok]

: The day Korean people are honored for their ancestors and prepare the harvesting food from the year. It's on August 15th in the lunar calrendar.

음력으로 8월 15일이며 추수에 대한 감사와 조상께 차례를 지내는 날

[eumnyeogeuro parwol sibo-ilimyeo chusu-e daehan gamsawa josangkke charyereul jinaeneun nal]

● 음식 [eumsik]

– 송편 [songpyeon]

– 식혜 [sik hye (sikye)]

– 수정과 [sujeonggwa]

● 추석 놀이 [chuseok nori]

– 강강수월래 [ganggang suwolrae]

: The women make a big circle, hold hands together and spin around. There is a special song called 'Gang Gang Suwolrae.'

여자들이 여럿이 둥글게 원을 만들고 '강강수월래' 라는 노래에 맞추어 빙글빙글 돌며 노는 놀이

[yeojadeuri yeoreosi dungeulge woneul mandeulgo 'gang gang suwolrae' raneun norae-e machu-eo bingeul bingeul dolmyeo noneun nori]

Korean Food •

한국 음식
hanguk eumsik

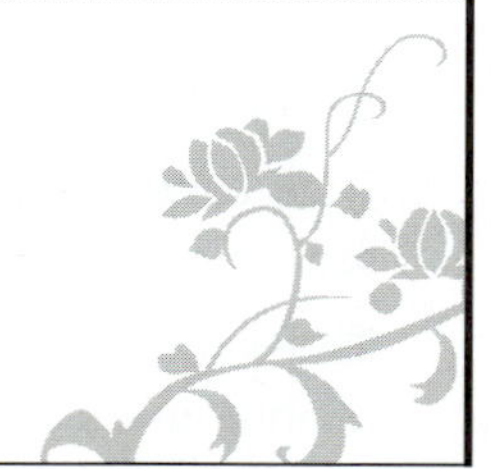

There are various kinds of food in Korea. Generally they are hot and spicy that bring out to the strong flavor of it. Now, I'd like to introduce to you those different types of Korean food.

한국에는 다양한 종류의 음식이 있다. 대체적으로 맵고, 뜨겁고, 강한 맛을 내는 것이 특징이다. 다음에서 다양한 한국의 음식을 소개한다.

[hangugeneun dayanghan jongnyui eumsigi itta. daechejeogeuro maepkko, tteugeopkko, ganghan maseul naeneun geosi teugjjing-ida. da-eumeseo dayanghan hangugui eumsigul sogaehanda]

● **Kimchi soup** 김치국 [kimchiguk]
: Chopped kimchi with plenty of water and boil
김치를 썰어 물을 많이 넣고 끓인 음식
[kimchireul sseoreo mureul mani neoko kkeurin eumsik]

● **Kimchi jjigae** 김치찌개 [kimchijjigae]
: Chopped kimchi with a little amount of water
김치를 썰어 물을 약간 넣고 끓인 음식
[kimchireul sseoreo mureul yakkan nectko kkeurin eumsik]

● **Bean sprout soup** 콩나물국 [kongnamulguk]
: Food goes with bean sprouts and boiling water
콩나물과 물을 넣어 끓인 음식
[kongnamulgwa mureul neo-eo kkeurin eumsik]

- **Tteok ppoki** 떡볶이 [tteokppoki]

  : Rice cake made of rice or flour stirred with Korean hot red bean paste and seasonings

  쌀이나 밀가루로 만든 떡을 고추장으로 양념하여 볶음

  [ssarina milkaruro mandeun tteogeul gochujangeuro yangnyeomhayeo bokkeum]

- **Kkag du gi** 깍두기 [kkagttugi]

  : Chopped radish in a square-shape mixed with red hot pepper powder and seasoning sauces

  무를 네모지게 썰어 고추가루와 양념을 버무려 만듦

  [mureul nemojige sseoreo gochugaruwa yangnyeomeul beomuryeo mandeum]

- **Tteog** 떡 [tteok]

  : Rice cakes made of rice

  쌀로 만든 한국 케이크의 일종

  [ssalro mandeun hanguk keikeu-ui iljjong]

- **Song pyeon** 송편 [songpyeon]

  : Rice cake dough with rice flour which is then made into different shapes and steamed

  쌀가루로 반죽을 하여 모양을 낸 후 쪄서 먹는 떡 (추석에 주로 먹음)

  [ssalkaruro banjugeul hayeo moyangeul naen hu jjyeoseo meongneun tteok. (chuseoge juro meogeum)]

- **Kkul tteok** 꿀떡 [kkultteok]

  : Rice cakes in a round shape with sugar or syrup which is then steamed

  쌀가루를 둥글게 모양을 내고 가운데에 설탕을 넣어 익힘

  [ssalkarureul dunggeulge moyangeul naego gaunde-e seoltangeul neo-eo ikim]

- **Tteog kkuk** 떡국 [tteogkkuk]

  : Sliced Rice cake in water and boiled broth

  쌀로 긴 가래떡을 만들어 썬 후 국을 끓여 먹음

  [ssalro gin garaetteogeul mandeureo sseon hu gugeul kkeuryeo meogeum]

  : Usually have on New Year's Day

새해 아침에 사골 국물에 끓여서 먹음
[saehae achime sagol gungmure kkeuryeoseo meogeum]

● Sun dae 순대 [sundae]

: A sausage made of bean curd and green-bean sprouts stuffed in pig intestine
돼지 창자에 채소와 당면을 넣어 만듦
[dwaeji changja-e chaesowa dangmyeoneul neo-eo mandeum]

● Pa Jeon 파전 [pajeon]

: Korean style pancake :food goes with green onion (scallion) and flour and then cook on a frying pan
파와 밀가루를 물에 섞어 프라이팬에 익힌 음식
[pawa milkkarureul mure sekkeo peura-i paene ikkin eumsik]

● Du bu 두부 [dubu]

: Ground beans boiled in water and squeezed
콩을 갈아서 만든 음식
[kongeul garaseo mandeun eumsik]

● Sun du bu 순두부 [sundubu]

: Soft tofu with various vegetables and then boiled.
연한 두부와 야채를 넣고 끓인 음식
[yeonhan dubuwa yachaereul neoko kkeurin eumsik]

● Sik hye 식혜 [sikye]

: Traditional sweetened beverage which is usually served on holidays
명절에 주로 먹는 달콤한 맛의 전통 음료
[myeongjeore juro meongneun dalkomhan mase jeontong eumnyo]

● Su jeong gwa 수정과 [sujeonggwa]

: Traditional sweet and spicy beverage which is usually served on hoidays
명절에 주로 먹는 달콤 매콤한 맛의 전통 음료
[myeongjeore juro meongneun dalkom maekomhan mase jeontong eumnyo]

● **Jap chae** 잡채 [japchae]

  : A mixed dish of vegetables and sliced meat.

  당면과 여러 가지 채소로 만든 음식

  [dangmyeongwa yeoreo gaji chaesoro mandeun eumsik]

● **Gal bi** 갈비 [galbi]

  : marinated and seasoned ribs of beef or pork

  소고기나 돼지고기를 여러 가지 양념으로 무쳐(재어)굽는 음식)

  [sogogina dwaejigogireul yeoreo gaji yangnyeomeuro mucheo(jae-eo) gumneun eumsik]

● **Bul go ki** 불고기 [bulgoki]

  : Roast meat; broiled(grilled)beef of pork (sliced and seasoned) which cook on the barbeque grill

  소고기나 돼지고기를 잘게 썰어 여러 가지 양념으로 무쳐(재어) 불판에 익힌 음식

  [sogogina dwaejigogireul jalge sseoreo yeoreo gaji yangnyeomeuro muchyeo(jae-eo) bulpane ikkin eumsik]

● **Sam gyeop sal** 삼겹살 [samgyeopsal]

  : Sliced boned pork rib (pork belly) which cook on the barbecue grill

  돼지고기를 얇게 썰어 팬에 구워 먹는 음식

  [dwaejigogireul yalke sseoreo paene guwo meongneun eumsik]

● **Gamja tang** 감자탕 [gamjatang]

  : Pork stew with bones of pork, potatoes, red hot bean pepper and various vegetables

  돼지고기와 돼지뼈, 통감자, 고추가루, 여러 가지 채소를 끓여 익힌 음식

  [doejigogiwa doejippyeo, tong-gamja, gochugaru, yeoreo gaji chaesoreul kkeuryeo ikin eumsik]

● **Sagol guk** 사골국 [sagolguk]

  : Korean traditional soup : made from bones from the four legs of a cow

  소의 다리뼈나 꼬리뼈를 물에 넣고 오래오래 끓인 음식

  [so-ui darippyeona kkorippyeoreul mure neoko orae orae kkeurin eumsik]

● **Bap** 밥 [bap]

: Cooked rice

쌀에 물을 넣어 익힌 음식

[ssare mureul neo-eo ikin eumsik]

● **Mi yeok kuk** 미역국 [miyeokkuk]

: Seaweed soup with beef. traditionally enjoyed on one's birthday

미역과 소고기로 끓인 국, 생일날 반드시 먹는 풍습이 있음

[miyeokwa sogogiro kkeurin guk, saeng-ilral bandeusi meongneun pungseubi isseum]

● **Seol leong tang** 설렁탕 [seolleongtang]

: Beef broth soup with green onion (scallion) and salt

소뼈를 고아서 만든 국에 파와 소금을 넣어 먹음

[soppyeoreul go-aseo mandeun guge pawa sogeumeul neo-eo meogeum]

● **Gal bi tang** 갈비탕 [galbitang]

: Boiled rib of beef in beef stock soup

소갈비를 넣고 끓인 음식

[Sogalbireul neoko kkeurin eumsik]

● **Kal guk su** 칼국수 [kalguksu]

: Hand made knife-cut noodles

밀가루를 물에 반죽한 후 칼로 썰어 물에 끓인 음식

[milkkarureul mure banjukan hu kalro sseoreo mure kkeurin eumsik]

● **Man du** 만두 [mandu]

: dumpling

밀가루를 반죽하여 겉을 만들고 그 안에 잘게 썬 고기와 김치를 넣어 만든 음식

[milkkarureul banjukayeo geoteul mandeulgo geu ane jalge sseon gogiwa gimchireul neo-eo mandeun eumsik]

● **Tteok Ra myeon** 떡라면 [tteongnamyeon]

: Stirred rice cake (tteok bok ki) and ramen (thin noodle) with red hot bean paste

떡볶이와 라면을 고추장에 버무려 볶은 음식

[tteokppokkiwa ramyeoneul gochujange beomu-yeo bokkeun eumsik]

● **Gim bap** 김밥 [gimppap]

: Rice rolled in dried laver, usually goes with pickled radish and spinach

밥에 참기름과 소금을 넣어 간을 한 후 단무지와 시금치 등을 넣어 김에 만 음식

[babe chamgireumgwa sogeumeul neo-eo ganeul han hu danmujiwa sigeumchi deung-eul neo-eo gime man eumsik]

● **So go gi kuk** 소고기국 [sogogikuk]

: Beef and radish soup

소고기와 무를 작게 썰어 끓인 국

[sogogiwa mureul jakke sseoreo kkeurin guk]

● **Kong na mul mu chim** 콩나물 무침 [kongnamul muchim]

: Boiled bean sprout seasoning with scallion and sesame oil

콩나물을 삶아 파와 참기름을 넣어 무친 음식

[kongnamureul ssalma pawa chamgireumeul neo-eo muchin eumsik]

● **Jeon** 전 [jeon]

: A panfried dish with vegetables in it

채소에 따라 전의 이름이 다양함

[chaeso-e ttara jeon-ui ireumi dayangham]

: It is named depending the shape of the vegetable

채소와 밀가루를 섞어 작게 모양을 만든 후 팬에 익힌 (지진) 음식

[chaesowa milkkarureul seokeo jakke moyangeul mandeun hu paene ikkin(jijin) eumsik]

● **Doen jang kuk** 된장국 [doenjangkuk]

: Boiled soup with soybean paste and vegetables

된장과 채소로 끓인 국

[doenjang-gwa chaesoro kkeurin guk]

● **Doen jang** 된장 [doengjang]

: Traditional soy bean paste which is naturally fermented

콩으로 만든 한국 전통 양념

[kong-euro mandeun hanguk jeontong yangnyeom]

● Go chu jang 고추장 [gochujang]

: Korean traditional seasoning sauces made of rice flour and red hot bean pepper.
The main ingredient and seasoning sauce of Korean dishes

쌀가루와 고추가루로 만든 한국 전통 양념. 한국 음식을 만드는 데 자주 사용됨

[ssakkaruwa gochukkaruro mandeun hanguk jeontong yangnyeom. Hanguk eumsigeul mandeu-neun de jaju sayongdoem]

Recipes of Korean Food

한국 음식 조리법

hanguk eumsik jorippeop

- **guk** 국 [guk]

  : Boiled soup or broth with plenty of water

  물을 많이 넣어 끓임

  [mureul mani neo-eo kkeurim]

- **muchida** 무치다 [무침_muchim]

  : The action of mixing well many ingredients

  재료를 골고루 섞음　예 김치를 무치다, 나물을 무치다

  [jaeryoreul golgoru seokkeum]

- **kkeurida** 끓이다 [끓임_kkeurim]

  : The action of bringing to boil cooking with plenty of water

  물을 많이 넣고 익히다

  [mureul mani neoko ikida]

- **jorida** 졸이다 [조림_jorim]

  : Boiling with plenty amount of water and boiling until liquid has almost evaporated.

  물을 많이 넣고 적어질 때까지 끓임

  [mureul mani neoko jeogeojil ttaekkaji kkeurim]

- **guda** 굽다 [구이_gu-i]

  : Fried or grilled directly on the barbecue grill

  팬이나 그릴 위에 직접 놓고 익힘

  [paenina geulil wi-e jikjeop noko ikim]

- **mandeulda** 만들다

  : Home made food

  손으로 직접 모양을 내서 만들다

  [soneuro jikjeop moyang-eul naeseo mandeulda]

  예 송편 [song pyeon], 만두 [man du]

- **twigida** 튀기다 [튀김_ twigim]

  : Fried with oil

  기름에 넣어 익히다　예 새우 튀김 [Saeu twigim], 야채 튀김 [yachae twigim]

  [gireume neo-eo ikida]

- **jaeda** 재다

  : Put in layers with various seasoning sauces for several hours

  여러 가지 양념에 재료를 몇 시간 섞어 놓음

  [yeoreo gaji yangnyeome jaeryoreul myeot sigan seokkeo no-eum]

- **goda** 고다, 우리다 [goda ; urida]

  : Soak out for a long time to make out the soup

  오래오래 끓여 국물을 내다　예 사골국 [sagol kuk], 곰탕 [gom tang]

  [orae orae kkeuryeo gungmureul naeda]

- **jjida** 찌다 [찜_ jjim]

  : Steam the food

  스팀으로 익힌 음식　예 떡 [tteok]

  [seutimeuro ikin eumsik]

- **bibida** 비비다 [비빔_ bibim]

  : Mixed various foods with a spoon

  여러 가지 재료를 숟가락을 이용하여 섞다　예 비빔밥 [bibim-pap]

  [yeoreo gaji jaeryoreul sukkarageul iyonghayeo seoktta]

- **boktta** 볶다 [볶음_bokkeum]

    : Fried vegetables and meat on the pan

    채소 또는 고기를 팬에 골고루 익힌 음식 예 김치 볶음밥 [kimchi bokkeumbap]

    [chaeso ttoneun gogireul paene golgoru ikin eumsik]

- **buchida** 부치다 [부침_buchim]

    : Vegetable(mixed with water) cooked on a griddle or fried

    채소에 물을 섞어 반죽하여 팬에 익힌 음식 예 파전 [pajeon], 부침 [buchim]

    [chaeso-e mureul seokkeo banjukayeo paen-e ikin eumsik]

- **tang** 탕 [tang]

    : Food that is soaked for a long time to make the soup

    고기나 뼈를 고아서 (우려서) 만든 음식 예 설렁탕 [seol reong tang] / 갈비탕 [galbi tang]

    [gogina ppyeoreul go-aseo mandeun eumsik]

- **banjuk** 반죽 [banjuk]

    : Handling the ingredients with a little amount of water

    재료를 물에 섞어 오래 주무름

    [jaeryoreul mure seokkeo orae jumureum]

- **beomurida** 버무리다

    : Mixed the food usually with hands

    골고루 섞다 (보통 손으로 섞음)

    [golgoru seoktta]

- **malda** 말다

    : Roll up the food

    음식을 싸다 예 김밥 [gim bap]

    [eumsigeul ssada]

- **ssam da** 삶다

    : Get the ingredient from the boiled water

    재료를 물에 끓여 건져냄 예 삶은 국수 [ssalmeun gukssu]

    [jaeryoreul mure kkeuryeo geonjyeonaem]

● **jijida** 지지다 [지짐_jijim]

: Sizzle the food with oil on both sides

팬에 기름을 넣고 음식을 앞 뒤로 익힘

[paene gireumeul neoko eumsigeul ap dwiro ikⁿm]

● **jji gae** 찌개 [jjigae]

: A pot stew with vegetable and water

채소와 물을 섞어 끓인 음식

[chaesowa mureul seokkeo kkeurin eumsik]

한국의 기념일

hangugui ginyeomil

● **March 1st Independence Movement Day** 삼일절 (3월 1일)
[sam il jeol (samwol i-ril)]

: The day people had a huge protest against Japanese Colonization
일본의 식민지에 대항하여 만세를 부른 날을 기념함
[ilbon-ui singminji-e daehanghayeo mansereul bureun nareul ginyeomham]

● **April fool's Day** 만우절 (4월 1일) [manujeol (sa wol iril)]

: You are officially allowed to tell a light joke or lie on this day
가벼운 농담이나 거짓말을 허용하는 날
[gabyeoun nongdamina geojinmareul heoyonghaneun nal]

● **Arbor Day** 식목일 (4월 5일) [sik mok il (= singmogil) sa wol o il]

: A day to encourage the planting of trees and flowers
나무를 심는 날
[namureul simneun nal]

● **Buddah's Birthday** 석가탄신일 (음력 4월 8일)
[seog ga tan sin il (lunar sawol paril)]

: Celebrate the birth of Buddah
석가의 생일을 기념하는 날
[seokka-ui saeng-ireul ginyeomhaneun nal]

● **Children's Day** 어린이 날 (5월 5일) [eorini nal (o-wol o il)]

: Have many events and give gifts for the children
어린이들을 위한 날
[eorinideureul wihan nal]

● **Parents' Day** 어버이날 (5월 8일) [eobeoi nal (o-wol paril)]

  : Appreciation for our parents' love

  부모님의 은혜에 감사 드리는 날

  [bumonim-ui eunhye-e gamsadeurineun nal]

● **Teacher's Day** 스승의 날 (5월 15일) [seuseung-ui nal (o-wol siboil)]

  : Appreciation for our teachers' love

  선생님의 은혜에 감사드리는 날

  [seonsaengnim-ui eunhye-e gamsadeurineun nal]

● **Memorial Day** 현충일 (6월 6일) [hyeonchungil (yuwol yugil)]

  : Make a token in honor of dying troops in Korean War

  6 · 25 전쟁 때 죽은 군인들을 기념하는 날

  [yuk·io jeonjaeng ttae jugeun gunindeureul ginyeomhaneun nal]

● **Constitution Day** 제헌절 (7월 17일) [je heon jeol (chirwol sipchril)]

  : A holiday to celebrate the proclamation of our national laws

  헌법을 제정한 날을 기념함

  [heonppeobeul jejeonghan nareul ginyeomham]

● **Independence Day** 광복절 (8월 15일) [gwangbokjeol (parwol siboil)]

  : Celebrate the day to be a free country from Japanese Colonization

  한국의 독립을 기념함

  [hangug-ui dongnibeul ginyeomham]

● **Military Day** 국군의 날 (10월 1일) [gukkun-ui nal (si wol iril)]

  : Have many events such as marching or parade for the Korean soldiers

  군인들을 위한 날

  [gunindeureul wihan nal]

● **National foundation Day** 개천절 (10월 3월) [gaecheonjeol (siwol samil)]

  : Celebrate the foundation of Korea

  한국의 개국 기념일

  [hangug-ui gaeguk ginyeomil]

● **Hangeul Proclamation Day** 한글날 (10월 9일) [hangeul nal (siwol guil)]

  : A celebration of the day "Hangeul" was invented

  한글 제정을 기념한 날

  [hangeul jejeong-eul ginyeomhan nal]

● **Christmas Day** 성탄절 (12월 25일) [seongtanjeol (sibiwol isiboil)]

  : Celebrate the birth of Jejus Christ

  예수의 생일을 기념함

  [yesu-ui saeng-ireul ginyeomham]

한국의 문화재

hangugui munhwajae

Korea's history is more than 5,000 years old.

한국의 역사는 오천 년 이상입니다.

[hangug-ui yeokssaneun ocheonnyeon isang-imnida]

● **남대문** [namdaemun]

: This is one of the most important heritage sites which is located in Seoul.

대한민국의 가장 중요한 문화재의 하나로 서울에 소재하고 있다.

[daehanmingug-ui gajang jungyohan munhwajae-ui hanaro seoure sojaehago itta]

: It is also called 'sungnyemun.'

'숭례문' 이라고도 한다.

[sung-rye-mun(sungnyemun) iragodo handa]

● **동대문** [dongdaemun]

: It has been built over 600 years and it was created to protect the capital, Seoul. Which has been stood as "The main gate of Yi(Lee) dynasty."

건축된 지 600년이 넘는 서울을 보호하기 위해 만든 조선시대의 성문. 보물 제 1호.

[geonchukdoen ji yookbaeknyeoni neomneun seoureul bohohagi wihae mandeun joseonsidae-ui seongmun. bomul je il-ho.]

: It is also called 'Heunginjimun.'

'흥인지문' 이라고도 한다.

['heung-injimun' iragodo handa]

● **경복궁** [gyeongbok gung]

: It was the most important royal palace during the Yi(Lee) dynasty. It is located in Seoul.

조선시대 궁궐 중 가장 중요한 의미를 지닌 궁궐로 서울에 자리하고 있다.

[joseonsidae gunggwol jung gajang jung-yohan uimireul jinin gung-gwolro seourae jarihago itta]

● 종묘 [jongmyo]

: It is a mounment for remembering emperors and and their wives in the royal family.

조선시대 역대 왕과 왕비 및 추존된 왕과 왕비의 신위를 모신 왕가의 사당

[joseonsidae yeokttae wanggwa wangbi mit chujondoeun wanggwa wangbi-ui sin-uireul mosin wangga-ui sadang]

: It is located in Jongro, Seoul

서울 종로에 위치하고 있다.

[Seoul jongno-e wichihago itta]

● 훈민정음 [hunminjeongeum]

: The Hunminjeongeum is the final edition of the text that was drafted by King Sejong to explain(the creation of) Hangeul.

조선 세종 28년(1446)에 창제된 한글의 제작 원리가 실린 책

[joseon Sejong isib-palnyeone changjedoen hangeul-ui jejak wolriga silrin chaek]

● 불국사 [bulguksa]

: It was registered with UNESCO in 1995. The temple is one of the famous temples in Korea . It is located in Gyungju, Gyeongsang province.

경상북도 경주에 있으며 한국의 대표적인 사찰의 하나로, 1995년 유네스코 세계문화유산 목록에 등록되었다.

[gyeongsangbukdo gyeongju-e isseumyeo hangug-ui daepyojeogin sachal-ui hanaro, cheon-gubaekgusibonyeon segyemunhwayusan mongnoge deungrok doe-eotta]

● 석굴암 [seokkuram]

: It was registered with UNESCO in 1995. It was constructed in Silla Dynasty.

신라시대에 건축 되었으며 경주 토함산에 위치하고 있고, 1995년 유네스코 세계문화유산 목록에 등록되었다.

[silla sidae-e geonchuk doe-eoseumyeo Gyeongju tohamsane wichihago ikko, 1995 nyeon segyemunhwayusan mongno-e deungrok doe-eotta]

● 다보탑 & 석가탑 [dabotap & seokkatab]

: It is the master hof stone tower of Silla Daynasty. It is located inside Bulkuk temple in Gyeongju.

경주 불국사 안에 위치하고 있으며 신라시대 탑의 양식을 잘 보여주고 있는 의미있는 문화재다.

[gyeongju bulkuksa ane wichihago isseumyeo sillasidae tab-ui yangsigeul jal boyeojugo inneun uimi inneun munhwajaeda]

● **수원화성** [suwon hwaseong]

: One of the beautiful fortresses from the Yi Dynasty. It is located in Suwon. It was registered with UNESCO in 1997.

조선시대 성곽 건축의 아름다움을 잘 간직한 건축굴로 경기도 수원에 위치하고 있다. 1997년 유네스코 세계문화유산으로 등록되었다.

[joseonsidae seonggwak geonchug-ui areumdaumeul jal ganjikan geonchugmulro gyeong-gido suwone wichihago itta. cheon-gubaekgusipchilnyeon uneseuko segyemunhwayusaneuro deungnok doe-eotta]

● **팔만 대장경** [palmandaejanggyeong]

: This is carved on the wooden panels which are about the Buddist bible. It is placed in Haein temple in hapcheon, GyeongNam.

경남 합천 해인사에 있는 팔만 대장경은 불교의 경전을 나무에 새겼으며 호국의 기원을 담고 있다.

[gyeongnam hapcheon hae-insa-e inneun palman daejanggyeongeun bulgyo-ui gyeongjeoneul namu-e saegyeosseumyeo hogug-ui giwoneul damkko itta]

● **고인돌** [goindol]

: It was registered in UNESCO on December, 2000. It shows a funeral ceremony in BC 2,000~3,000.

BC 2,000~3,000년 전의 장례와 무덤의식을 보여주며, 2000년 12월 유네스코 세계문화유산으로 지정되었다.

[BC icheonyeon~samcheonyeon jeon-ui jangnyewa mudeom-uisigeul boyeojumyeo, icheonyeon sibiwol uneseuko segyemunhwayusaneuro jijeongdoe-eotta]

한국의 가족 호칭

hangugui gajok hoching

- **mother** 어머니 [eo-meo-ni (eomeoni)]

- **mom** 엄마 [eom-ma (eomma)]

- **father** 아버지 [a-beo-ji (abeoji)]

- **dad** 아빠 [a-ppa (appa)]

- **grandfather [father's father [polite]]** 할아버님 [hal-a-beo-nim (harabeonim)]

- **grandpa** 할아버지 [hal-a-beo-ji (harabeoji)]

- **grandmother [father's mother [polite]]** 할머님 [hal-meo-nim (halmeonim)]

- **grandma [father's mother [normal]]** 할머니 [hal-meo-ni (halmeoni)]

- **mother's mother [mother's mother]** 외할머니 [oe-hal-meo-ni]

- **mother's father [mother's father]** 외할아버지 [oe-hal-a-beo-ji]

- **husband's mother** 시어머니 [si-eo-meo-ni]

- **husband's father** 시아버지 [si-a-beo-ji]

- **husband's brother** 아주버님 [a-ju-beo-nim]

- **husbad's sister** 애기씨 [ae-gi-ssi]

- **father's elder brother [uncle]** 큰 아버지 [keun-a-beo-ji]

- **father's youger brother [uncle]** 작은 아버지 [jag-eun-a-beo-ji]

- **father's brother [not marriage]** 삼촌 [samchon]

- **father's sister** 고모 [go-mo]

- **younger brother** 남동생 [nam-dong-saeng]

- **younger sister** 여동생 [yeo-dong-saeng]

- **elder brother** 형, 형님 [hyeong or hyeong-nim]

- **mother's sister** 이모 [i-mo]

- **mother's brother [uncle]** 외삼촌 [oe-sam-chon]

- **mother and father'a brother or sister's children** 사촌 [sa-chon]

- **oldest son** 장남, 큰 아들 [jang-nam, keun-a-deul]

- **second son** 차남, 둘째 아들 [cha-nam, dul-jjae-a-deul]

- **oldest daughter** 장녀, 큰 딸 [jang-nyeo, keun-ttal]

- **second daughter** 차녀, 둘째 딸 [cha-nyeo, dul-jjae-ttal]

- **daughter** 딸 [ttal]

- **son** 아들 [a-deul]

- **daughter [son]'s daughter** 손녀 [son-nyeo]

- **daughter [son]'s son** 손자 [son-ja]

* Traditionally it's common in Korea that you don't call the names of parents or grandparents' names but call them with the family names.
한국에서는 보통 부모의 이름을 부르지 않고 엄마(mom), 아빠(cad)라 부른다.
[hangugeseoneun botong bumo-ui ireumeul bureuji anko 'eomma', 'appa' ra bureunda]

The General Naming in Korea •

일반 호칭

ilban hoching

- **new born baby, toddler, baby (born ~ 12 month)** 아기, 애기 [a-gi, ae-gi]
- **infants [12month~ 3 Years]** 영아 [yeong-a]
- **children [3 years ~ 5 Years]** 유아 [yu-a]
- **children [Male & Female : 6 years~12 Years]** 아동 [a-dong]
- **boy [Male :13 Years ~ 18 Years] Male** 소년 [so-nyeon]
- **girl [Female :13 Years ~ 18 Years]** 소녀 [so-nyeo]
- **boyfriend** 남자친구 [nam-ja-chin-gu]
- **girlfriend** 여자친구 [yeo-ja-chin-gu]
- **lover** 연인 [yeon-in]
- **honey [between a husband and a wife]** 여보 [yeo-bo] / 당신 [dangsin]
- **sweet heart [between loves]** 자기 [ja-gi]
- **you [friends or the one younger]** 너 [neo]
  [between about the same ages :
  NEVER use for the elder or older people] 당신 [dang-sin]
- **daughter** 딸 [ttal]
- **son** 아들 [a-deul]

- **father's daughter** 손녀 [son-nyeo]

- **father's son** 손자 [son-ja]

- **sir [title for the elder]** 어르신 [eo-reu-sin]

- **friend [every age]** 친구 [chingu]

- **woman [30s~]** 여자 [yeo-ja]

- **man [30s~]** 남자 [nam-ja]

- **lady [20s~30s]** 숙녀 [suk-nyeo] / 아가씨 [a-ga-ssi]

- **young** 젊은 [jeol-meun]

- **old** 늙은 [neul-geun]

- **kindergarten [attending between 3~6 year-old]**
  유치원 [yu-chi-won]

- **preschool, day care center [attending between 1~5 year-old]**
  어린이집 [eo-rin-i-jib (eorinijib)]

- **woman** 아주머니(아줌마) [ajumeoni (ajumma)]

- **old lady** 할머니 [hal-meo-ni]

- **young man** 청년 [cheongnyeon] / 젊은이 [jeol-meun-i]

- **man** 아저씨 [a-jeo-ssi]

- **old man** 할아버지 [hal-a-beo-ji(harabeoji)]

- **guys [=] folks [usually when you call the younger people]**
  너희들 [neo-hi-deul]

- **ladies and gentlemen** 여러분 [yeo-reo-bun]

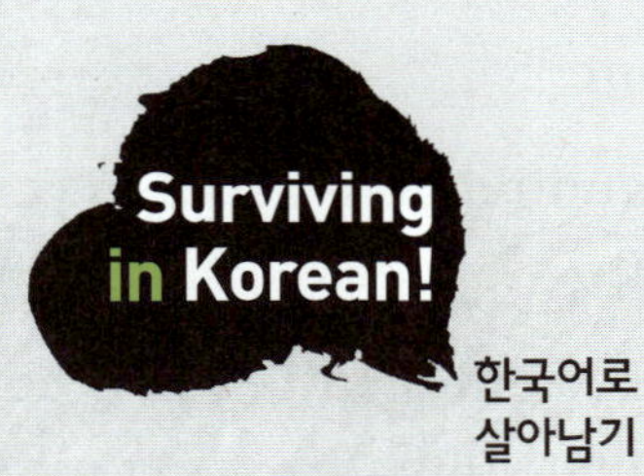
Surviving
in Korean!
한국어로
살아남기

Crawling to Korean

한국어로 기어가기

hagugeoro gi-eogagi

대명사: 인칭, 지시

daemyeongsa : inching, jisi

01 | I | 나, 1인칭
na, irinching

- **I am _____.** 나는 ______입니다. [naneun ________ imnida]
- **I am a girl.** 나는 소녀입니다. [naneun sonyeo-imnida]
- **I am a student.** 나는 학생입니다. [naneun haksaeng-imnida]
- **I am a mother.** 나는 엄마입니다. [naneun eomma-imnida]
- **I am a Korean.** 나는 한국인입니다. [naneun hanguginimnida]
- **I am 40 years old.** 나는 마흔 살입니다. [naneun maheunsarimnida]
- **I am healthy.** 나는 건강합니다. [naneun geonganghamnida]
- **I am happy.** 나는 행복합니다. [naneun haengbokamnida]

02 | You | 너, 당신, 2인칭
neo, or dangsin, iinching

- **You are _________.** 당신은 ____입니다. [dangsineun ______ imnida]
- **You are a man.** 당신은 남자입니다. [dangsineun namja-imnida]
- **You are a president.** 당신은 사장입니다.
  [dangsineun sajang-imnida]
- **You are a father.** 당신은 아버지입니다.
  [dangsineun abeoji-imnida]

- **You are a Canadian.** 당신은 캐나다 사람입니다.
  [dangsineun kaenada saramimnida]

- **You are kind.** 당신은 친절합니다. [dangsineun chinjeoramnida]

- **You are slim.** 당신은 날씬합니다. [dangsineun nalssinhamnida]

- **You are great.** 당신은 훌륭합니다.
  [dangsineun hulryunghamnida]

03 He | 그, 그 남자, 3인칭   geu, or geu namja, saminching

- **He is ________.** 그는 ______일니다. [geuneun ________ imnida]

- **He is a boy.** 그는 소년입니다. [geuneun sonyeonimnida]

- **He is an actor.** 그는 배우입니다. [geuneun bae-u-imnida]

- **He is young.** 그는 젊습니다. [geuneun jeomseumnida]

- **He is American.** 그는 미국 사람입니다.
  [geuneun miguk saramimnida]

- **He is good looking.** 그는 잘 생겼습니다.
  [geuneun jal saenggyeosseumnida]

- **He is honest.** 그는 정직합니다. [geuneun jeongjikamnida]

04 She | 그녀, 그 여자, 3인칭   geunyeo, geu yeoja, saminching

- **She is ________.** 그녀는 ______입니다.
  [geunyeoneun ________ imnida]

- **She is a lady.** 그녀는 숙녀입니다. [geunyeoneun sungnyeo-imnida]

- She is cute. 그녀는 귀엽습니다. [geunyeoneun gwiyeopsseumnida]

- She is a professor. 그녀는 교수입니다. [geunyeoneun gyosu-imnida]

- She is hard working. 그녀는 열심히 일합니다.
[geunyeoneun yeolsimi iramnida]

- She is a younger sister. 그녀는 내 여동생입니다.
[geunyeoneun nae yeodongsaeng-imnida]

05 It: 3rd person's singular | 그것 (3인칭 단수)
geugeot (saminching dansu)** dansu: 3rd person's singular

- It is __________. 그것은 ______입니다. [geugeoseun ______ imnida]

- It is a cellular phone. 그것은 휴대폰입니다.
[geugeoseun hyudaeponimnida]

- It is huge. 그것은 큽니다. [geugeoseun keumnida]

- It is foggy. 안개가 끼었습니다. [angaega kkiyeosseumnida]

- It is noon. 낮 열두 시입니다. [nat yeol dusi-imnida]

- It is late. 늦었습니다. [neujeosseumnida]

06 They: 3rd person's plural | 그들, 그것들 (3인칭 복수)
geudeul, geugeotdeul, saminching boksu

- They are ______. 그들은, 그것들은 ______입니다.
[geudeureun, geugeodeureun ______ imnida]

- They are family. 그들은 가족입니다. [geudeureun gajogimnida]

- **They are brave.** 그들은 용감합니다. [geudeureun yong-gamhamnida]

- **They are pencils.** 그것들은 연필입니다.
  [geugeotteureun yeonpirimnida]

- **They are fast.** 그것들은 빠릅니다. [geugeodeureun ppareumnida]

- **They are necessary.** 그것들이 필요합니다.
  [geugeottri piryohamnida]

07 This | 이것, 단수   *igeot , dansu*

- **This is ______.** 이것은 ______입니다. [igeoseun ______ imnida]

- **This is a cup.** 이것은 컵입니다. [igeoseun keobimnida]

- **This is milk.** 이것은 우유입니다. [igeoseun uyu-imnida]

08 These | 이것들은*, 복수   *igeotdeureun, boksu*

* more frequently use in : botong, igeoseun i ra go sa yong ham ni da
보통 '이것은' 이라고 사용합니다

- **These are____.** 이것들은 ______입니다. [igoetteureun ____ imnida]

- **These are strawberries.** 이것들은 딸기입니다.
  [igeotteureun ttalgi-imnida]

- **These are flowers.** 이것들은 꽃입니다. [igeotteureun kkochimnida]

- **That is ______.** 저것은 ___입니다.

  [jeogeoseun ________ imnida]

- **That is a map.** 저것은 지도입니다.
  [jeogeoseun jido-imnida]

- **That is a police officer.** 저 사람은 경찰관입니다.
  [jeo sarameun gyeongchalgwanimnida]

10 Those | 저것들은*, 복수

jeogeodeureun*, boksu

* more frequently use in 저것은(Jeogeoseun)
  보통 '저것은' 이라고 사용합니다. botong jeogeoseun irago sayonghamnida

- **Those are ______.** 저것들은 ___입니다. [Jeogeotteureun ___ imnida]
- **Those are ants.** 저것들은 개미입니다. [Jeogeotteureun gaemi-imnida]
- **Those are books.** 저것들은 책입니다. [Jeogeotteureun chaegimnida]
- **Those are trees.** 저것들은 나무입니다. [Jeogeotteureun namu-imnida]

11 There | 거기, 저기   geogi, jeogi

- **There is ______.** 거기 ______있습니다. [geogi ________ isseumnida]
- **There is a book.** 거기에 책이 있습니다. [geogi-e chaegi isseumnida]
- **I will be there.** 거기에 있을게요. [geogi-e isseulkkeyo]

- **There are many apples.** 거기에 사과가 많이 있습니다.
  [geogi-e sagwaga mani isseumnida]

- **There are buses and taxies.** 저기에 버스와 택시가 있습니다.
  [jeogi-e beoseuwa taekssiga isseumnida]

- **There it is.** 저기에 있어요.
  [jeogi-e isseoyo]

A marker •

조사 : ~은, 는, 이, 가

josa : ~eun, ~neun, i, ga

 Use of | '~은, 는, 이, 가' 의 사용

'eun, neun, i, ga' ui sayong

The marker ~은, ~이 are followed by ending consonant sounds of the words.

The marker ~가, ~는 are followed by ending vowel sounds of the words .

A: What's your name? 이름은 무엇입니까? [ireumeun mu-eosimnikka]

B: My name is Iris. 제 이름은 아이리스 입니다. [je ireumeun airiseu-imnida]

A: How old are you? 몇 살 입니까? [myeotssal imnikka]

B: I am 20 years old. 저는 스무 살입니다. [jeoneun seumu sarimnida]

A: When's your birthday? / When were you born?
생일이 언제입니까? [saeng-iri eonje-imnikka]

B: I was born in summer.
내 생일은 여름입니다. [nae saeng-ireun yeoreumimnida]

A: Is it raining? 비가 내립니까? [biga naerimnikka]

B: It's raining. 비가 내립니다. [biga naerimnida]

Section 03

Possessive

소유격 : ~의

soyukkyeok : ~ui

01 Possessive Marker 소유격 soyugyeok 'ui'

To indicate one's possession which is usually followed by subject.

~의 [ui]

A: What do you do for a living? 당신의 직업은 무엇입니까?
[dansgsin-ui jigeobeun mu-eosimnikka]

B: I'm a singer. 나의 직업은 가수입니다. [na-ui jigeobeun gasu-imnida]

A: Who is she? 그녀는 누구입니까? [geunyeoneun nugu-imnikka]

B: She's my sister. 나의 언니입니다. [na-ui eonni-imnida]

A: What's that? 저것은 무엇입니까? [jeogeoseun mu-eosimnikka]

B: That's my car. 나의 차입니다. [na-ui cha-imnida]

목적격 : ~을, 를

mokjeokkyeok : ~eul, reul

01 **Objective | 목적격**   *mokjeokkyeok 'eul, reul'*

Use of ~을, 를

A: What are you doing now? 지금 무엇을합니까?
[jigeum mueoseul hamnikka]

B: I am reading a book. 책을 읽습니다. [chaegeul iksseumnida]
I'm having some rice. 밥을 먹습니다. [babeul meoksseumnida]
I am studying. 공부를 합니다. [gongbureul hamnida]

A: Which season do you like? 어떤 계절을 좋아하세요?
[etteon gyejeoreul joahaseyo]

B: I like spring. 봄을 좋아합니다. [bomeul joahamnida]

A: Which singer do you like? 어떤 가수를 좋아하세요?
[etteon gasureul joahaseyo]

B: I like 'Rain(Bi)'. 가수 '비' 를 좋아합니다. [gasu 'Bi' reul joahamnida]

A: What kind of songs do you like? 어떤 노래를 좋아하세요?
[eotteon noraereul joahaseyo]

B: I like R& B. R&B를 좋아합니다. [R&B reul joahamnida]

긍정, 부정대답

geungjeong, bujeong daedap

01 | **Yes, No Questions** | 긍정, 부정대답

A: Are you a Korean? 당신은 한국 사람 입니까?
[dangsineun hanguk saramimnikka]

B: Yes, I am a Korean. 예, 한국 사람입니다. [ye, hanguk saram-imnida]

A: Is that blue? 저것은 파란색입니까? [jeogeoseun paransaek-imnikka]

B: No, it's not. It's green. 아니오, 그것은 초록색입니다.
[aniyo, geugeoseun chorokssaek-imnida]

A: Do you like bread? 당신은 빵을 좋아하십니까?
[dangsineun ppang-eul joahamnikka]

B: Yes, I do. 예, 저는 빵을 좋아합니다.
[ye, jeoneun ppang-eul joahamnida]

A: Do yoy have an American friend? 미국인 친구가 있습니까?
[migugin chinguga isseumnikka]

B: No, I don't. 아니오, 없습니다. [aniyo, eopsseumnida]

This is designating the place and time with a noun : ～에 [~e]
This place marker indicates where an action happens : ～에서 [~eseo]

A: **Where do you go?** 어디에 갑니까? [eodi-e gamnikka]
B: **I go to school.** 학교에 갑니다. [hakkyo-e gamnida]

A: **Where is it?** 어디에 있어요? [eodi-e isseoyo]
B: **It's on the desk.** 책상 위에 있습니다. [chaekssang wi-e isseumida]

A: **Where are you from?** 어느 나라에서 오셨습니까?
[eoneu nara-eseo ossyeosseumnikka]
B: **I'm from Korea.** 한국에서 왔어요.
[hangugeseo wasseoyo]

A: **Where shall we meet?** 어디에서 만나요?
[eodi-eseo mannayo]
B: **Let's meet at a station.** 정거장에서 만나요.
[jeonggeojang-eseo mannayo]

A: **What do you do in the evening?** 저녁에 뭐 하세요?
[jeonyeoge mwo haseyo]
B: **I have an engagement in the evening.** 저녁에 약속이 있습니다.
[jeonyeoge yakssogi isseumnida]

한국어로 걸음마 05

hangugeoro georeumma

Section 01

기본적인 인사표현을 익힌다

gibonjeogin insa pyohyeoneul ikinda

---

01 | Hi! | 만났을 때 — mannasseul ttae

When you greet the people who are younger than you are or between friends.

● Hi!

안녕!
[annyeong]
: Between friends or, younger than you are

● Hello !

안녕하세요?
[annyeonghaseyo]
: When you greet the people who are older, polite way of greeting

● How are you (doing)?

안녕하십니까?
[annyeonghasimnikka]
: More polite way to greet than "hello"

● How's your family?

가족들은 어떻게 지내요?
[gajokdeureun eotteoke jinaeyo]
: When you greet and regard family members

- **It's nice meeting you.**

  (= I'm glad to meet you, pleasure to meet you.)

  처음 만났을 때

  [cheo-eum mannasseul ttae]
  : When you meet a person very first time

  처음 뵙겠습니다.

  [cheo-eum boepgesseumnida]

  만나서 반갑습니다.

  [mannaseo bangapsseumnida]

- **Do I know you?**

  (= Have we met before?)

  전에 만난 적 있지요?

  [jeone mannan jeok ijjiyo]

  어디서 많이 뵌 분 같아요.

  [(=) eodiseo mani boen bun gatayo]
  : When you recognize the person who you have met before

- **May I have your business card?**

  명함 한 장 주시겠어요?

  [myeongham han jang jusigesseoyo]
  : When you ask for the namecard

- **I wanted to see you**

  (= I have been looking forward to seeing you.)

  만나 뵙고 싶었습니다.

  [manna boepkko sipeosseumnida]
  : When you express to the person who you've heard and longing to meet

02   Bye | 헤어질 때   *he-eojil ttae*

When you say "good bye"

- ## Bye

  안녕~

  [annyeong]

  : When you say "good bye"

- ## When you say "good bye"

  잘가~

  [jalga]

- ## More polite than "an nyeong"

  안녕히 계세요.

  [annyeonghi gyeseyo]

- ## The most polite

  안녕히 계십시오.

  [annyeonghi gyesipsiyo]

- ## See you later , take care (of yourself)

  또 만나자.

  [tto mannaja]

  또 만나.

  [tto manna]

  다음에 뵙겠습니다. [da-eume boepgesseumnida]
  When you expect to see each other in near future you can also say "good bye or bye"

  몸 조심하세요. [mom josimhaseyo]
  Most polite way of "tto manna"

● **Excuse me.**
(=pardon me, sorry to bother you, sorry to interrupt you)
실례합니다.
[silrye hamnida]

● **I'm sorry .(= I apologize ~)**
미안합니다.
[mianhamnida]
죄송합니다.
[(=) joesonghamnida]

● **That's O.K.**
No problem.
Never mind.
Not at all.
It's doesn't matter.
I don't care.
괜찮습니다.
[gwaenchansseumnida]
상관없습니다.
[(=) sanggwan-eopsseumnida]

● **I appreciate ~**
Thank you.
감사합니다.
[gamsahamnida]

고맙습니다.
[(=) gomapsseumnida]

- **Thanks a lot.**

  Thank you so much.

  Thanks a million.

  Many thanks.

  I really appreciate~

  정말 감사합니다.
  [jeongmal gamsahamnida]

  정말 고맙습니다.
  [(=) jeongmal gomapsseumnida]

 **04** **Getting to know each other** | 개인적인 질문을 할 때
gae-injeogin jilmuneul hal ttae

- **Where are you from?**

  어디(어느 나라)에서 오셨어요?
  [eodi(eoneu nara)eseo osyeosseoyo]

- **Where do you live?**

  어디에서 사세요?
  [eodi-eseo saseyo]

- **What's your name?**

  (= May I have your name please?) (= Did I get your name?)

  이름이 뭐에요?
  [ireumi mwoyeyo]

- ### How old are you?
  몇 살이에요?
  [myeot ssal iyeyo]

- ### When were you born?
  몇 년 생이에요?
  [myeon nyeon saeng-iyeyo]

- ### When is your birthday?
  생일이 언제세요?
  [saeng-iri eonjeseyo]

- ### What's your hobby?
  취미가 뭐세요?
  [chwimiga mwoseyo]

- ### What are you doing over weekends?
  주말에는 보통 어떻게 지내세요?
  [jumareneun botong eotteoke jinaeseyo]

- ### What do you want to be?
  장래희망이 무엇입니까?
  [jangnaehimang-i mu-eosimnikka]

- ### What are your wishes?
  희망이 무엇입니까?
  [himang-i mu-eosimnikka]

- ### How many people are in your family?
  ### (= Do you live with your family?)
  가족이 어떻게 되세요?
  [gajogi eotteoke doeseyo]

- **What's your blood type?**
혈액형이 무엇입니까?
[hyeoraekyeongi mu-eosimnikka]

- **What do you do for a living?**
  (= What's your job (occupation)?)
무슨 일 하세요?
[museun il haseyo]

- **What kind of food do you like?**
어떤 음식을 좋아하세요?
[eotteon eumsigeul joahaseyo]

- **Are you an outgoing person?**
적극적인 성격입니까?
[jeokkeugjeogin seonggyeogimnikka]

- **Do you like any sports?**
운동 좋아하세요?
[undong joahaseyo]

- **Do you like movies?**
영화 좋아하세요?
[yeonghwa joahaseyo]

- **Do you like rainy days?**
비 오는 날 좋아하세요?
[bi oneunnal joahaseyo]

- **What seasons do you like?**
어떤 계절을 좋아하세요?
[eotteon gyejeoreul joahaseyo]

● **How's the weather in your country?**
당신 나라의 날씨는 어떻습니까?
[dangsin nara-ui nalssineun eotteosseumnikka]

● **Where is your hometown?**
고향이 어디십니까?
[gohyang-i eodisimnikka]

● **What's your phone number?**
전화번호가 어떻게 됩니까?
[jeonhwabeonhoga eotteoke doemnikka]

05 Introduce Oneself | 자기 소개 *jagi sogae*

● **Hi, How are you doing?**
안녕하세요?
[annyeonghaseyo]

● **Nice to meet you. (= Glad to meet you)**
만나서 반갑습니다.
[mannaseo bangabseupnida]

● **I am Kara. (= My name is Kara)**
제 이름은 카라입니다.
[je ireumeun kara-imnida]

● **I am Korean.**
나는 한국사람입니다.
[naneun hanguksaram-imnida]

- **I live in Seoul.**
  나는 서울에 살고 있습니다.
  [naneun Seoure salgo isseumnida]

- **There are four people in my family.**
  우리 가족은 네 명입니다.
  [uri gajogeun ne myeong-imnida]

- **My dad is a teacher.**
  아버지는 선생님입니다.
  [abeojineun seonsaengnim-imnida]

- **My mom is a housewife.**
  어머니는 주부입니다.
  [eomeonineun jubu-imnida]

- **My sister has been married.**
  언니는 결혼을 했습니다.
  [eonnineun gyeoroneul haesseumnida]

- **My younger brother is a college student. (= My younger brother goes to college.)**
  남동생은 대학생입니다.
  [namdongsaengeun daehakssaeng-imnida]

- **I am an artist.**
  나는 화가입니다.
  [naneun hwaga-imnida]

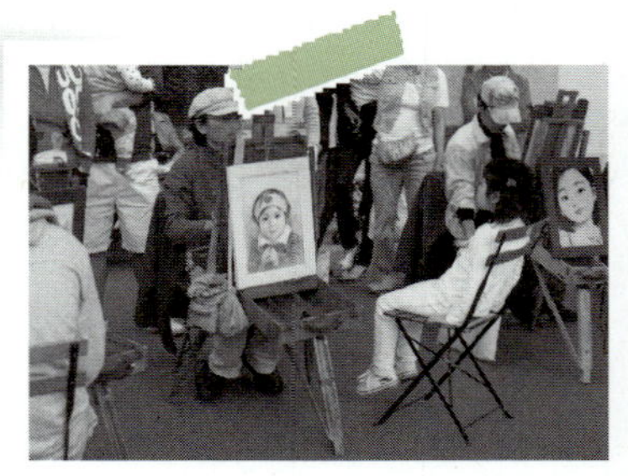

- **I am not married. (= I am single.)**
  나는 결혼을 하지 않았습니다.
  [naneun gyeoroneul haji anasseumnida]

● **I want to get married next year.**

내년에는 결혼을 하고 싶습니다.
[naenyeoneneun gyeoroneul hago sipsseumnida]

● **I have a lot of friends.**

나는 친구들이 많습니다.
[naneun chingudeuri mansseumnida]

● **I love reading.**

나는 책읽기를 좋아합니다.
[naneun chae-ilkkireul joahamnida]

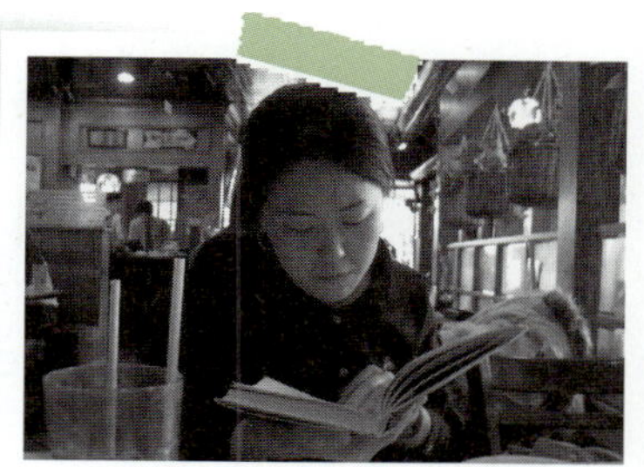

● **My hobby is traveling.**

여행을 좋아합니다.
[yeohaengeul joahamnida]

● **I am outgoing.**

나는 성격이 명랑합니다.
[naneun seongkkyeogi myeongnang-hamnida]

● **I want to travel around the world.**

나는 세계 여행을 하고 싶습니다.
[naneun segye yeohaengeul hago sipsseumnida]

06 Meeting | 만났을 때   manasseul ttae

● **Where are you from?**

어디에서 오셨습니까?
[eodi-eseo ossyeosseumnikka]

- **How is the weather in Korea?**

  한국의 날씨는 어떻습니까?

  [hankug-ui nalssineun eotteosseumnikka]

- **What country are you from?**

  어느 나라에서 오셨습니까?

  [eoneu nara-eseo osyeosseumnikka]

- **I am from Korea.**

  한국에서 왔습니다.

  [hangugeseo wasseumnida]

- **How many family members do you have?**

  가족이 몇 명입니까?

  [gajogi myeot myeong-imnikka]

- **How many children do you have?**

  아이들이 몇 명 있습니까?

  [aideuri myeot myeong isseumnikka]

- **I have two children.**

  두 명의 아이가 있습니다.

  [du myeong-ui aiga isseumnida]

- **Do you have any children?**

  자녀가 있습니까?

  [janyeoga isseumnikka]

- **Will you be the long?**

  여기 오래 계실 겁니까?

  [yeogi orae gyesil geomnikka]

- **Are you free this evening?**

  오늘 저녁에 시간 있으세요?

  [oneul jeonyeoge sigan isseuseyo]

- **I'd like to invite you to dinner this evening.**

  오늘 저녁 식사에 당신을 초대하고 싶어요.

  [oneul jeonyeok siksa-e dangsineul chodaehago sipeoyo]

- **I am glad to see you.**

  만나 뵙게 되어 반갑습니다.

  [manna boepge doe-eo bangapsseumnida]

- **Would you like something to drink?**

  마실 것 드릴까요?

  [masil geot deurilkkayo]

- **Where is the washroom?(= restroom, bathroom)**

  화장실은 어디입니까?

  [hwajangsireun eodi-imnikka]

- **Please, pass me the pepper.**

  후추를 건네 주세요.

  [huchureul geonne juseyo]

- **The food is delicious.**

  음식이 참 맛있습니다.

  [eumsigi cham masisseumnida]

- **I enjoyed this evening very much.**

  오늘 저녁 매우 즐거웠습니다.

  [oneul jeonyeok mae-u jeulgeowosseumnida]

- **Thank you for inviting.**
초대해 주셔서 감사합니다.
[chodaehae jusyeoseo gamsahamnida]

- **See you again.**
또 만나요.
[tto mannayo]

07 Phone call | 전화 걸 때   *jeonhwa geol ttae*

- **Hello, this is __________.**
안녕하세요? 저는 ________ 입니다.
[annyeonghaseyo? jeoneun ________ imnida]

- **May I speak to ________?**
________와 통화를 하고 싶습니다.
[________wa tonghwareul hago sipsseumnida]

- **Who is speaking, please. (= Who is calling, please?)**
누구십니까?
[nugusimnikka]

- **I can't hear you very well.**
잘 안 들립니다.
[jal an deulrimnida]

- **Please, try again.**
다시 걸어 주세요.
[dasi georeo juseyo]

● **She is not here right now. (= She is away from her desk now.)**
그녀는 지금 여기에 없습니다.
[geunyeoneun jigeum yeogi-e eopseumnida]

● **Just a moment, please. (= Hold on, please.)**
잠시만 기다려 주세요.
[jamsiman gidaryeo juseyo]

● **I'll call you again. (= I'll call again later.)**
다시 전화하겠습니다.
[dasi jeonhwa hagesseumnida]

● **Thank yoy for calling.**
전화 주셔서 감사합니다.
[jeonhwa jusyeoseo gamsahamnida]

● **What is your telephone number?**
전화 번호가 어떻게 되세요?
[jeonhwa beonhoga eotteoke doeseyo]

● **Is there any message?**
(= Do you want to leave a message?)
전할 말씀이 있으세요?
[jeonhal malsseumi isseuseyo]

● **Will you have him to call me back, please?**
전화 좀 걸어달라고 전해 주시겠어요?
[jeonhwa jom georeodalrago jeonhae jusigesseoyo]

● **I'll tell him as soon as he comes.**
그 분이 오시는 대로 전하겠습니다.
[geu buni osineun daero jeonhagesseumnida]

- **This is _________ speaking. (= This is she.)**
  제가 _______입니다.
  [jega _______imnida]

- **Let me have the phone number.**
  전화 번호를 알려 주세요.
  [jeonhwa beonhoreul alryeo juseyo]

08 Daily Routine | 하루 일과   *haru ilgwa*

- **What time do you usually get up in the morning?**
  아침에 주로 몇 시에 일어나십니까?
  [achime juro myeotssi-e ireonasimnikka]

- **How do you go to school / work?**
  학교(직장)에 어떻게 가십니까?
  [hakkyo-e(jikjjange) eotteoke gasimnikka]

- **How long does it take to get there?**
  시간이 얼마나 걸립니까?
  [sigani eolmana geolrimnikka]

- **How do you like your work?**
  당신의 일이 즐겁습니까?
  [dangsin-ui iri jeulgeopsseumnikka]

- **What subject do you like the most?**
  어떤 과목이 가장 재미있습니까?
  [eotteon gwamogi gajang jaemi-isseumnikka]

What time is your lunch break?

점심 식사 시간이 언제입니까?

[jeomsim sikssa sigani eonje imnikka]

Do you have a cellular phone?

휴대폰이 있습니까?

[hyudaeponi isseumnikka]

How much water do you drink a day?

하루에 물을 얼마나 드십니까?

[haru-e mureul eolmana deusimnikka]

What do you usually do after school / work?

방과 후 / 퇴근 후에는 주로 어떤 일을 하십니까?

[banggwa hu / toegeun hu-eneun juro etteon ireul hasimnikka]

How often do you dine out?

얼마나 자주 외식을 하십니까?

[eolmana jaju oesigeul hasimnikka]

What time do you go to bed?

몇 시에 주무세요?

[myeot ssi-e jumuseyo]

How many phone calls do you make a day?

전화를 얼마나 여러 번 하세요?

[jeonwhareul eolmana yeoreo beon haseyo]

Line up. (= Stand in line.)

줄 서세요.

[jul seoseyo]

- **I didn't mean to hurt you.**
  마음 아프게 하려던 건 아니었어요.
  [ma-eum apeuge haryeodeon geon ani-eosseoyo]

- **Open it up.**
  열어 보세요.
  [yeoreo boseyo]

09 | Appearance & Characters | 외모와 성격
oemowa seonkkyeok

- **Be in a good shape.**
  몸매를 유지하다.
  [mommaereul yujihada]

- **Got a sense of fashion.**
  패션 감각이 좋군요.
  [paesyeon gamgagi jokunyo]

- **fashionable**
  옷 입은 게 멋진
  [ot ibeun ge meotjjin]

- **short / small / tiny**
  작은
  [jageun]

- **tall**
  키가 큰
  [kiga keun]

- **beautiful / gorgeous / awesome / great**
  아름다운, 멋진
  [areumdaun, meotjjin]

- **attractive / charming / graceful / elegant**
  매력적인, 우아한
  [maeryeokjjeogin, uahan]

- **sexy / hot**
  섹시한
  [ssekssihan]

- **pretty**
  예쁜
  [yeppeun]

- **cute**
  귀여운
  [gwiyeo-un]

- **cool**
  멋진, 성격 좋은
  [meotjjin, seongkkyeok jo-eun]

- **classical / antique**
  고전적인
  [gojeonjeogin]

- **naive**
  순진한
  [sunjinhan]

- **gentle / tender**
  부드러운
  [budeureoun]

- **manners / behave**
  예의 바른
  [ye-ui bareun]

- **intelligent / bright**
  지적인
  [jijjeogin]

- **sharp / mean**
  냉정한
  [naengjeonghan]

- **sulky / mean / nasty**
  못된
  [mottoen]

- **handsome / cute**
  잘 생긴
  [jal saenggin]

- **neat / tidy**
  단정한
  [danjeonghan]

- **get an attitude**
  반항적인
  [banhangjeogin]

● humanistic / warm-hearted / kind
따뜻한 마음을 가진
[ttatteutan ma-eumeul gajin]

● enthusiastic / emotional / passionate
열정적인
[yeoljjeongjeogin]

● **You are such a chicken.**
겁장이, 비열한
[geopjangi, biyeolhan]

● **You are so cheap.**
소심한
[sosimhan]

10 | Agreement and Disagreement | 동의 그리고 반대
dong-ui geurigo bandae

● **That's a good idea.**
그거 좋은 생각입니다.
[geugeo jo-eun saenggagimnida]

● **I think so, too.**
저도 그렇게 생각합니다.
[jeodo geureoke saenggakamnida]

● **That's what I thought.**
제 말씀이 바로 그겁니다.
[je malsseumi baro geugeomnida]

● **I agree.**

동의해요. 같은 생각이에요.
[dong-uihaeyo, gateun saenggagiyeyo]

● **You're right. (= You can say that again.)**

당신 말이 맞아요.
[dangsin mari majayo]

● **You may be right.**

당신이 옳을 겁니다.
[dangsini oreul geomnida]

● **That may be true.**

그게 맞을 거예요.
[geuge majeul geoyeyo]

<table>
<tr><td>11</td><td>When you greet people | 내방객 응대하기
naebanggaek eungdaehagi</td></tr>
</table>

● **Please, welcome.**

방문을 환영합니다.
[bangmuneul hwanyeonghamnida]

● **How may I help you? (= What can I do for you?)**

무얼 도와 드릴까요?
[mueol dowa deurilkkayo]

● **Please, wait a second.**

잠시 기다려 주세요.
[jamsi gidaryeo juseyo]

- **Please follow me.**
  저를 따라 오세요.
  [jeoreul ttara oseyo]

- **This way, please.**
  이 쪽으로 오세요.
  [i jjogeuro oseyo]

- **Please, go ahead.**
  먼저 가시지요.
  [meonjeo gasijiyo]

- **Please, come in.**
  들어 오세요.
  [deureo oseyo]

- **Please, have a seat. (= Please, take a seat.)**
  앉으세요.
  [anjeuseyo]

- **I hope to see you again.**
  다시 만나기를 바랍니다.
  [dasi managireul baramnida]

12   Essential Expressions | 자주 쓰는 표현
jaju sseuneun pyohyeon

- **Well**
  음~
  [eum~]

- **Here you go.**
  여기 있습니다.
  [yeogi isseumnida]

- **Here we are.**
  도착했어요.
  [dochakaesseoyo]

- **Shall we go?**
  갈까요?
  [galkkayo]

- **There you go.**
  잘 하네요.
  [jal haneyo]

- **There you are.**
  그렇죠.
  [geureochyo]

- **Here you are.**
  여기 있어요.
  [yeogi isseoyo]

- **Here it is.**
  여기 있어요.
  [yeogi isseoyo]

- **Here I am.**
  나, 여기 있어요.
  [na, yeogi isseoyo]

- **I love it.**
  좋아요.
  [joayo]

- **I like it.**
  좋아요.
  [joayo]

- **Ummmmm. (when you think about something.)**
  음~~~~
  [eum]

- **I guess.**
  아마도
  [amado]

- **I think.**
  아마도
  [amado]

- **I believe.**
  내 생각엔
  [nae saeng-ga-en]

- **That's great.**
  좋군요.
  [jokunyo]

- **That's all right.**
  괜찮아요.
  [gwaenchanayo]

- **I think so.**
  내 생각도 같아요.
  [nae saenggaktto gatayo]

- **Have a nice day.**
  좋은 하루 되세요.
  [jo-eun haru doeseyo]

- **Have a great trip back.**
  여행 잘 하고 오세요.
  [yeohaeng jal hago oseyo]

- **Can I bring~?**
  가져 와도 되나요?
  [gajyeo wado doenayo]

- **Get well soon.**
  빨리 나으세요.
  [ppalri na-euseyo]

- **That's it.**
  그것 뿐이에요.
  [geugeot ppunieyo]

- **What do you want?**
  무얼 원하세요?
  [mu-eol wonhaseyo]

- **Be careful.**
  조심하세요.
  [josimhaseyo]

- **Hopefully**
바라건대
[barageondae]

- **I understand.**
이해합니다.
[ihaehamnida]

- **Do you know where__________?**
여기가 어디에요?
[yeogiga eodiyeyo]

- **I miss you.**
보고 싶어요.
[bogo sipeoyo]

- **What do you think __________?**
어떻게 생각하세요?
[eotteoke saenggakaseyo]

- **How do you say __________?**
__________을 어떻게 말합니까?
[__________eul eotteoke maramnikka]

- **Did you have / eat __________?**
__________을 드셨습니까?
[__________eul deusyeosseumnikka]

- **How's your day?**
어떻게 지내셨어요?
[eotteoke jinaesyeosseoyo]

- **Did you have a nice day?**
오늘 하루 어떠셨어요?
[oneul haru eotteosyeosseoyo]

- **Let's go. / Take off.**
갑시다.
[gapssida]

- **Super / excellent / great / marvelous**
최고입니다.
[choego-imnida]

- **Thanks for your treat.**
잘 먹었습니다.
[jal meogeosseumnida]

- **Thanks for the meal.**
잘 먹었습니다.
[jal meogeosseumnida]

- **It's on me. (= Let me take the tab.)**
제가 낼게요.
[jega naelgeyo]

- **Enjoy (your meal).**
맛있게 드세요.
[masikke deuseyo]

- **Hold on (second).**
잠시만요.
[jamsimanyo]

- **Wait up!**
  잠깐만요!
  [jamkkanmanyo]

- **Don't hang up! (= Hold in a line.)**
  끊지 말고 기다리세요.
  [kkeunji malgo gidariseyo]

- **One by one**
  차례 차례
  [charye charye]

- **Anyway**
  어쨌든
  [eojjaetteun]

- **I got it. (= I see.)**
  알았어요.
  [arasseoyo]

- **Don't do that!**
  하지 마세요!
  [hajimaseyo]

- **Stop doing that!**
  그만 하세요!
  [geuman haseyo]

- **Maybe**
  아마도
  [amado]

● **Do you want to join us?**
함께 하실래요?
[hamkke hasilraeyo]

● **You don't need to __________ .**
_______할 필요 없어요.
[_______hal piryo eopsseoyo]

● **Let's take a seat. (= Have a seat.)**
앉으세요.
[anjeuseyo]

● **It's yummy. (= It's delicious.)**
맛있어요.
[masisseoyo]

● **The food is great(here).**
음식 참 훌륭하군요.
[eumsik cham hulryunghagunyo]

● **How's your flight?**
비행기 여행 어떠셨어요?
[bihaengi yeohaeng eotteosyeosseoyo]

● **Did you have a nice / pleasant trip?**
여행 즐거우셨어요?
[yeohaeng jeulgeo-usyeosseoyo]

감정 표현

gamjeong pyohyeon

01 When you get angry | 화가 났을 때 hwaga nasseul ttae

● **Are you okay?**
괜찮아요?
[gwaenchanayo]

● **Are you all right?**
괜찮으세요?
[gwaenchaneuseyo]

● **What's wrong? (= What's the matter with you?)**
무슨 일이죠?
[museun irijo]

● **Is something wrong with you?**
뭐 잘못된 일이라도 있으세요?
[mwo jalmottoen irirado isseuseyo]

● **I'm mad. (= I'm pissed off.)**
나, 엄청 화났어요.
[na, eomcheong hwanasseoyo]

● **I'm disappointed.**

실망했어요.
[silmanghaesseoyo]

● **I can't stand it anymore.**
더 이상 참을 수 없어요.
[deo isang chameul ssu eopsseoyo]

● **This isn't my day. (= This is such a long day.)**
오늘 안 좋은 날이예요.
[oneul an jo-eun nariyeyo]

● **That's too bad.**
안 됐군요.
[an doekkunyo]

● **Be cool (= Chill out, take it easy)**
진정하세요.
[jinjeonghaseyo]

02 When you are happy | 기쁠 때 *gippeul ttae*

When you are happy

● **I'm happy.**
행복합니다.
[haengbokamnida]

● **I'm very glad. (= I'm very pleased.)**
저는 기뻐요.
[jeoneun gippeoyo]

● **I am hilarious.**
좋아 죽겠어요.
[joa jukkesseoyo]

● **I made my day. (= Such a lucky day.)**

운 좋은 날이었어요.

[un jo-eun narieosseoyo]

● **I feel excellent. (= I feel great. I feel good.)**

기분 최고예요.

[gibun choegoyeyo]

● **I am up in the air. (= I'm in the seventh heaven.)**

날아갈 것 같아요.

[naragal geot gattayo]

● **I'm satisfied.**

만족합니다.

[manjokamnida]

● **Great**

좋아요, 훌륭해요.

[joayo, hulryunghaeyo]

● **Pretty good**

괜찮아요.

[gwaenchanayo]

● **Good**

좋아요.

[joayo]

● **That's great.**

그것 참 좋군요.

[geugeot cham jokunyo]

- **That's amazing.**

대단하네요.

[daedanhaneyo]

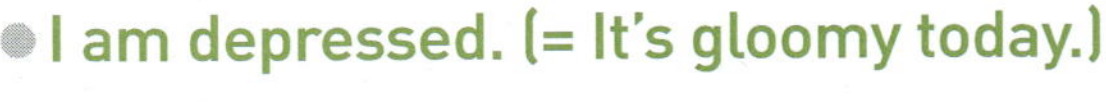

- **I am sad.**

슬퍼요.

[seulpeoyo]

- **I am depressed. (= It's gloomy today.)**

우울해요.

[u-uraeyo]

- **I am exhausted.**

지쳤어요.

[jichyeosseoyo]

- **I'm not feeling well. (= I don't feel good.)**

몸이 안 좋아요.

[momi an joayo]

- **I am overwhelmed.**

일 때문에 지쳤어요.

[il ttaemunae jichyeosseoyo]

- **I am mad. (= I am upset.)**

정말 화 났어요.

[jeongmal hwa nasseoyo]

- **I'm pissed off.**
  화나서 미치겠어요.
  [hwanaseo michigesseoyo]

- **It's such a long day. (= It's a tough day.)**
  힘든 하루였어요.
  [himdeun haruyeosseoyo]

- **I am puzzled.**
  당황됩니다.
  [danghwang doemnida]

- **I am scared.**
  무서워요.
  [museowoyo]

- **I got a shock. (= I'm shocked.)**
  충격적이었어요.
  [chunggyeokjjeogi-eosseoyo]

- **I got stressed.**
  스트레스 받아요.
  [seuteuresseu badayo]

- **I burst in tears.**
  눈물을 터뜨렸습니다.
  [numureul teotteuryeosseumnida]

- **I feel shamed.**
  창피해요.
  [changpihaeyo]

- **I don't know what to do.**
  어떻게 해야할지 모르겠어요.
  [eotteokke hae-yahalji moreugesseoyo]

- **I regret.**
  후회합니다.
  [huhoe-hamnida]

- **I feel sorry for~**
  유감입니다.
  [yugam-imnida]

- **I can't believe what happened.**
  믿어지지가 않아요.
  [mideojijiga anayo]

- **I got set up.**
  결국 이거였군요.
  [gyeolguk igeo-yeokkunyo]

- **No way!**
  말도 안돼요.
  [maldo andwaeyo]

- **I'm anxious. (= I am worried.)**
  걱정 돼요.
  [geokjjeong dwaeyo]

- **It was touching.**
  감동 받았어요.
  [gamdong badasseoyo]

- **I give up.**
  포기했어요.
  [pogi-haesseoyo]

- **Don't stop believing. (= Never give up.)**
  잘 할 수 있어요.
  [jal hal su isseoyo]

- **I stopped believing.**
  믿을 수 없어요.
  [mideul su eopsseoyo]

장소 표현
jangso pyohyeon

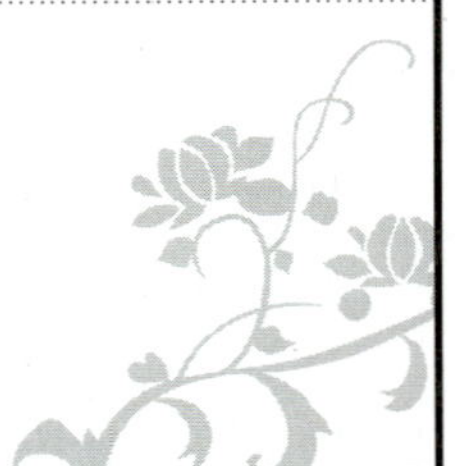

---

01   At a Restaurant | 식당에서   sikttang-eseo

● **Is any Korean restaurant around here?**
이 근처에 한국 식당이 있나요?
[i geuncheo-e hanguk sikttangi innayo]

● **Which way to go?**
어디로 가야 하나요?
[eodiro gaya hanayo]

● **A table for five, please.**
5인용 테이블 부탁합니다.
[o-inyong te-ibeul butakamnida]

● **Are you ready to order?**
무엇을 주문하시겠어요?
[mu-eoseul jumunhasigesseoyo]

● **Can I have a menu, please?**
메뉴판 주세요.
[menyupan juseyo]

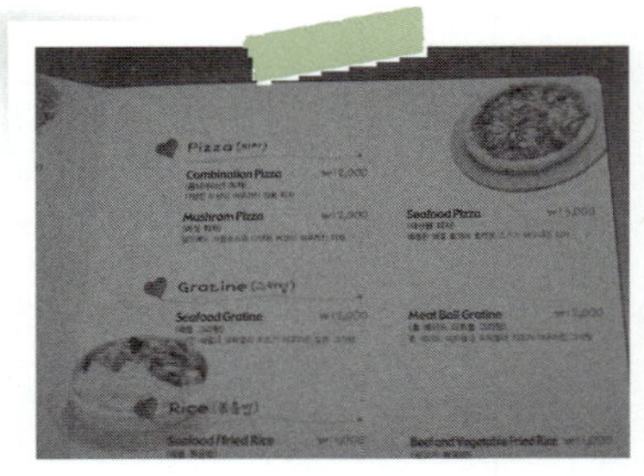

● **Here is the menu.**
여기 메뉴가 있습니다.
[yeogi menyuga isseumnida]

- ### What kind of food do you like?
  어떤 음식을 드시겠어요?
  [eotteon eumsigeul deusigesseoyo]

- ### Do you like hot and spicy food?
  매운 음식 좋아하세요?
  [mae-un eumsik joahaseyo]

- ### Would you like some meat?
  고기 드시겠어요?
  [gogi deusigesseoyo]

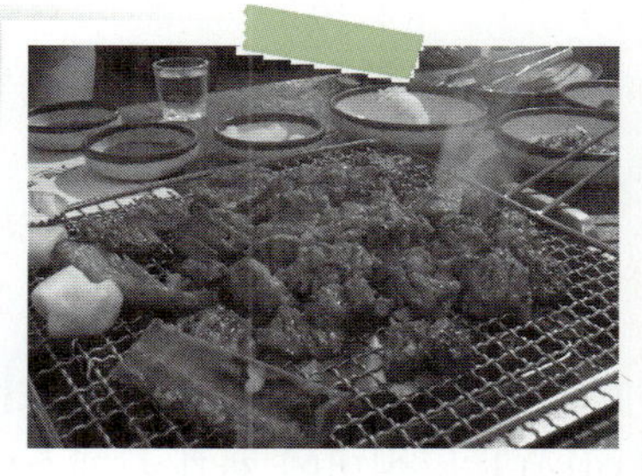

- ### How about fish?
  생선은 어떠세요?
  [saengseoneun eotteoseyo]

- ### How do you like this dish?
  이 음식은 어때요?
  [i eumsigeun eottaeyo]

- ### I will have Kimchi Jjigae.
  김치찌개를 먹겠습니다.
  [kimchijjigaereul meokkesseumnida]

- ### It smells good.
  냄새가 참 좋습니다.
  [naemsaega cham josseumnida]

- ### How did you like the food?
  음식 맛이 어떠셨어요?
  [eumsik masi eotteosyeosseoyo]

- **How do you like your coffee?**
  (= How do you like your coffee, with cream or sugar?)
  커피에 크림과 설탕을 넣으시겠어요?
  [keopi-e keurimgwa seoltang-eul neo-eu-sigesseoyo]

- **I'll have my coffee black.**
  블랙 커피로 하겠습니다.
  [beulraek keopiro hagesseumnida]

- **It's on me.**
  계산은 제가 할게요.
  [gyesaneun jega halkkeyo]

- **No, not at all. It's on me this time.**
  아닙니다. 이번엔 제가 사겠습니다.
  [animnida. ibeonen jega sagesseumnia]

- **Can I have check, please?**
  계산서 주세요.
  [gyesanseo juseyo]

- **Do you take credit cards? (= Do you take plastic?)**
  카드로 계산됩니까?
  [cadeuro gyesandoemnikka]

- **May I have a receipt, please.**
  영수증 주세요.
  [yeongsujeung juseyo]

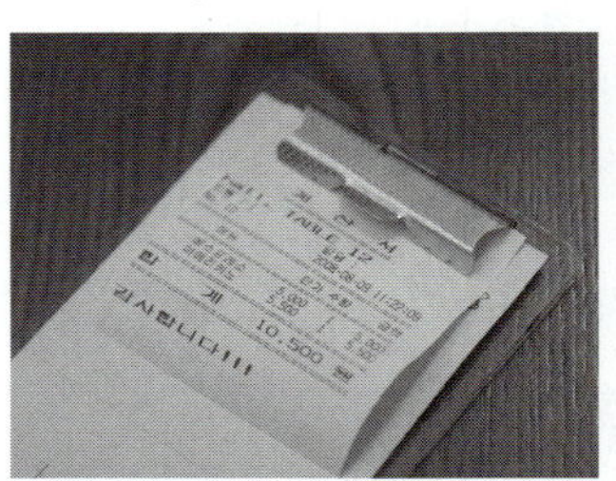

- **The food is great in this restarurant.**
  이 식당 음식 참 맛있습니다.
  [i sikttang eumsik cham masisseumnida]

- **Korean food is so delicious.**
한국 음식은 참 맛있군요.
[hanguk eumsigeun cham massikkunyo]

- **Thanks for the meal, it's great.**
음식, 참 맛이 있었습니다.
[eumsik, cham masi isseosseumnida]

- **Thank you for the meal, today.**
잘 먹었습니다.
[jal meogeosseumnida]

- **Why don't you have some more?**
더 드세요.
[deo deuseyo]

- **I'm full.**
배 부릅니다.
[bae bureumnida]

- **I'm enough. (= I really enjoyed the meal.)**
충분히 먹었습니다
[chungbuni meogeosseumnida]

02 At a Shopping Center | 시장에서　　sijang-eseo

- **How can I get to Namdaemun markets?**
남대문 시장이 어디입니까?
[namdaemun sijangi eodi-imnikka]

● **Are there a lot of things to buy?**

물건이 많이 있습니까?

[mulgeoni mani isseumnikka]

● **Are the things inexpensive?**

물건 값은 쌉니까?

[mulgeon gabseun ssamnikka]

● **How much is this?**

이것은 얼마입니까?

[igeoseun eolma-imnikka]

● **Can I get some discount?**
(=) Can you make a better price?

깎아 주세요.

[kkakka juseyo]

● **Can you show me that one, please.**

저것도 보여 주세요.

[jeogeotto boyeo juseyo]

● **Is it good on me?**

내게 잘 어울립니까?

[naege jal eo-ulrimnikka]

● **Can I try this one?**

이 옷 입어볼 수 있습니까?

[i ot ibeobol ssu isseumnikka]

● **Where is the fitting room?**

옷 갈아 입는 곳이 어디입니까?

[ot gara imneun gosi eodi-imnikka]

- **I will take it.**
  그것 주세요.
  [geugeot juseyo]

- **How much are they?**
  얼마입니까?
  [eolma-imnikka]

- **Yes, can I get a receipt, please.**
  네, 영수증 주세요.
  [ne, yeongsujeung juseyo]

- **Thank you.**
  잘 봤습니다.
  [jal bwasseumnida]

- **I'll see you again.**
  다음에 올게요.
  [da-eume olkkeyo]

03 At a Bank | 은행에서   *eunhaeng-eseo*

In Korea, when you are at a bank, first you have to take a numbered ticket and then you go to the bankteller when your number is lit.

With a bankteller

- **May I open the new account? (= I'd like to open the new account?)**
  통장을 만들고 싶습니다.
  [tongjang-eul mandeulgo sipsseumnida]

- **Can I apply for an automatic payment plan?**
자동 이체 신청을 하고 싶어요.
[jadong iche sincheong-eul hago sipeoyo]

- **Can I apply for a telebanking plan?**
텔레뱅킹 신청해 주세요.
[telebaenking sincheonghae juseyo]

- **Can you give me cash, please?**
현금으로 주세요.
[hyeongeumeuro juseyo]

- **Can you cash this check?**
수표를 현금으로 바꾸고 싶어요.
[supyoreul hyeongeumeuro bakkugo sipeoyo]

현금지급기

- **Please, insert the card.**
카드를 넣어 주세요.
[kadeureul neo-eojuseyo]

- **Press the PIN number.**
비밀 번호를 누르세요.
[bimil beonhoreul nureuseyo]

- **Press the "OK" button.**
확인 버튼을 누르세요.
[hwagin beoteuneul nureuseyo]

● **Get your transaction slip.**

명세표를 받으세요.

[myeongsepyoreul badeuseyo]

● **Ask for the bankteller.**

직원에게 문의하세요.

[jigwonege munihaseyo]

04　At a Department Store ｜ 백화점에서

baekhwajeom-eseo

● **How do I get to the department store?**

백화점은 어디로 갑니까?

[baekwajeomeun eodiro gamnika]

● **Where can I buy ties?**

넥타이를 사려면 어디로 가야 합니까?

[nekta-ireul saryeomyeon eodiro gaya hamnikka]

● **Can you show it to me?**

그것 보여 주시겠어요?

[geugeot boyeo jusigesseoyo]

● **Is there any color?**

다른 색상은 없습니까?

[dareun saekssangeun eopsseumnikka]

● **It's a bit small.**

사이즈가 좀 작네요.

[ssaijeuga jom jangneyo]

- **I will take it.**
  이것으로 살게요.
  [igeoseuro salkkeyo]

- **Can you wrap it up?**
  포장해 주시겠어요?
  [pojanghae jusigesseoyo]

- **Where are the restrooms?**
  화장실은 어디입니까?
  [hwajangsireun eodi-imnikka]

- **Which card has the discount?**
  할인되는 카드는 어떤 것입니까?
  [harin doeneun kadeuneun eotteon geot imnikka]

- **How much is it?**
  얼마입니까?
  [eolma-imnikka]

- **Where can I take a subway?**
  지하철 타려면 어떻게 합니까?
  [jihacheol taryeomyeon eotteoke hamnikka]

- **I'm looking for customer service center.**
  고객 서비스 센터는 어디입니까?
  [gogaek sseobisseu ssenteoneun eodi-imnikka]

● **What time do you go to work and finish at work?**

출근과 퇴근 시간이 언제입니까?

[chulgeungwa toegeun sigani eonjeimnikka]

● **How much will I earn?**
(= What about your income?) (= What is the salary?)

월급이 얼마입니까?

[wolgeubi eolma-imnikka]

● **Will I work 5 days a week?**

주 5일 일 하나요?

[ju oil il hanayo]

● **Is there any overtime work?**

시간 외 근무를 합니까?

[sigan oe geunmureul hamnikka]

● **What is the length of the contract?**

계약은 몇 년으로 합니까?

[gyeyageun myeon nyeoneuro hamnikka]

● **Does your company cover the 4 insurances?**

4대 보험은 가입해 줍니까?

[sadae boheomeun gaipe jumnikka]

● **I am leaving for the day earlier.**

먼저 퇴근하겠습니다.

[meonjeo toegeunhagesseumnida]

- **I don't feel good today.**
  몸이 좀 안 좋아요.
  [momi jom an joayo]

- **Can I call in sick?**
  조퇴하고 싶어요.
  [jotoehago sipeoyo]

- **See you tomorrow.**
  내일 뵙겠습니다.
  [naeil boegesseumnida]

- **I'll see you next Monday.**
  다음 주 월요일에 뵙겠습니다.
  [da-eumju woryoire boegesseumnida]

- **Have a nice vacation.**
  휴가 잘 지내세요.
  [hyuga jal jinaeseyo]

06   At an Airport | 공항에서   *gonghang-eseo*

- **Where can I take the buses?**
  버스는 어디에서 탑니까?
  [beoseuneun eodi-eseo tamnikka]

- **How much is the fare? (= What's the bus fare?)**
  요금이 얼마입니까?
  [yogeumi eolma-imnikka]

- **Round tickets, please.**

  왕복표 주세요.

  [wangbokpyo juseyo]

- **Where can I take the bus to go __________?**

  ________가는 버스는 _______에서 탑니까?

  [________ ganeun beoseuneun ________ eseo tamnikka]

- **How long does it take?**

  시간이 얼마나 걸립니까?

  [sigani eolmana geolrimnikka]

- **Where is the baggage claim?**

  수하물 센터는 어디입니까?

  [suhamul senteoneun eodi-imnikka]

- **Would you drop me off ________?**

  ________에서 내려 주세요.

  [________ eseo naeryeo juseyo]

- **Where is the foreign currency exchange center?**

  환전 센터는 어디입니까?

  [hwanjeon senteoneun eodiimnikka]

- **What is the foreign currency exchange rate?**

  환율이 어떻게 됩니까?

  [hwanyuri eotteokke doemnikka]

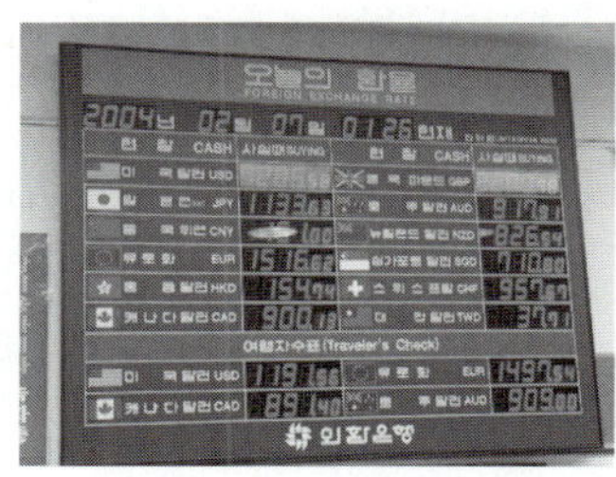

- **Is there an internet place?**

  인터넷 사용은 어디서 합니까?

  [inteonet sayongeun eodiseo hamnikka]

● **Where is the lost and found center?**

분실물 센터는 어디입니까?

[bunsilmul senteoneun eodiimnikka]

● **How do I get to the Gimpo airport?**

김포 공항까지는 어떻게 갑니까?

[gimpo gonghangkkajineun eotteoke gamnikka]

<table>
<tr><td>**07**</td><td>**At a Pub, Cafe and Bar** | 술집에서</td><td>*suljjip-eseo*</td></tr>
</table>

● **Which one do you want to drink?**
  (= What do you feel like to drink?)

어떤 술 드실래요?

[eotteon sul deusilraeyo]

● **What do you want for the side dishes?**

안주는 무엇으로 하시겠어요?

[anjuneun mueoseuro hasigesseoyo]

● **Do you have draft beer?**

생맥주 있어요?

[saengmaekjju isseoyo]

● **Do you have bottled beer?**

병맥주 있어요?

[byeongmaekjju isseoyo]

● **Can I have a bottle opener, please?**

병따개 주세요.

[byeongttagae juseyo]

- **What kind of alcohol do you have?**

어떤 종류의 술이 있나요?

[eotteon jongnyu-ui suri innayo]

- **One bottle, please.**

한 병 주세요.

[han byeong juseyo]

- **Can I have some water, please?**

물 좀 주세요.

[mul jom juseyo]

- **May I smoke here?**

담배 피워도 됩니까?

[dambae piwodo doemnikka]

- **Can I borrow a lighter? (= Do you get some light?)**

불 좀 빌려 주시겠어요?

[bul jom bilryeo jusigesseoyo]

- **What time do you close?**

몇 시까지 합니까?

[myeot sikkaji hamnikka]

- **May I have some tissues?**

휴지 좀 주세요.

[hyuji jom juseyo]

- **Check, please. (= Bill, please.)**

계산서 주세요.

[gyesanseo juseyo]

● **I'm looking for a restroom, please.**

화장실은 어디인가요?

[hwajangsireun eodiingayo]

● **Coffee, please.**

커피 주세요.

[keopi juseyo]

08   **At a Movie, Concert and Musical | 영화관, 콘서트, 뮤지컬**

yeonghwagwan, konsseoteu, myujikeol

● **What time does it start?**

몇 시에 시작하나요?

[meot ssie sijakanayo]

● **Two tickets, please.**

표 두 장 주세요.

[pyo du jang juseyo]

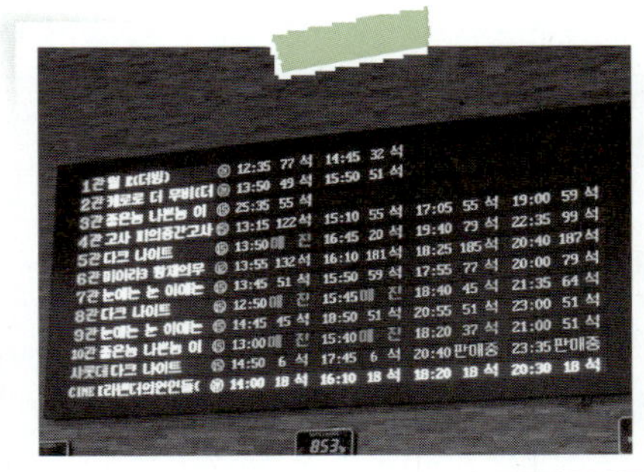

● **How much is it?**

얼마입니까?

[eolma-imnikka]

● **Back row, please.**

뒷 좌석으로 주세요.

[dwit jwaseogeuro juseyo]

● **Is this movie good?**

이 영화 재미있습니까?

[i yeonghwa jaemiisseumnikka]

- **Do you have an English caption?**
  영어 자막이 있습니까?
  [yeong-eo jamagi isseumnikka]

- **Which cards cover the discount payment?**
  할인되는 카드는 어떤 겁니까?
  [harindoeneun kadeuneun eotteon geomnikka]

- **Can I get refund?**
  환불은 됩니까?
  [hwanbureun doemnikka]

- **Can I get an exchange?**
  교환 됩니까?
  [gyohwan doemnikka]

- **What time is the matinee?**
  조조는 몇 시 입니까?
  [jojoneun myeot ssi imnikka]

- **What time does the last movie run?**
  마지막 영화는 몇 시에 합니까?
  [majimak yeonghwaneun myeot ssie hamnikka]

- **Is there any recession?**
  중간 휴식 시간이 있습니까?
  [junggan hyusik sigani isseumnikka]

- **I want to go the concerts.**
  콘서트에 가고 싶습니다.
  [konsseoteu-e gago sipsseumnida]

- **Who is singing at the concert?**

누구의 콘서트 입니까?

[nugu-ui konsseoteu imnikka]

- **How was the concert?**

콘서트는 어떠셨어요?

[konsseoteuneun eotteosyeosseoyo]

- **It was a fantastic concert. (= I've ever seen before.)**

정말 대단한 무대였어요.

[jeongmal daedanhan mudaeyeosseoyo]

- **Would you go to see the "Fever of Saturday Night"?**

"토요일 밤의 열기" 보러 가시겠어요?

["toyoil ppam-ui yeolgi" boreo gasigesseoyo]

- **Do I need to be dressed up?**
  (= Is there any proper dress required?)

어떤 복장이 좋을까요?

[eotteon bokjjangi jo-eulkkayo]

- **Let's meet in front of the theater.**

극장 앞에서 만나요.

[geukjjang apeseo mannayo]

- **The actors and actress' performed very well.**

배우들의 연기가 매우 좋았습니다.

[baeudeur-ui yeongiga maeu joasseumnida]

- **Thanks for taking me here.**

덕분에 잘 보았습니다.

[deokppune jal boasseumnida]

At a Hospital 병원에서 byeongwon-eseo

● **Where is the receptionist?**
접수하는 곳이 어디입니까?
[jeopssuhaneun gosi eodimnikka]

● **I have a pain here. (= It's painful here.)**
여기가 아파요.
[yeogiga apayo]

● **I hurt my legs.**
다리를 다쳤어요.
[darireul dachyeosseoyo]

● **I have a headache.**
머리가 아파요.
[meoriga apayo]

● **I have a fever.**
열이 있어요.
[yeori isseoyo]

● **I'm dizzy.**
어지러워요.
[eojireowoyo]

● **I have a stomachache.**
배가 아파요.
[baega apayo]

● I've been throwing up. (= I've been vomitting.)
계속 토해요.
[gyesok tohaeyo]

● I have diarrhea.
설사를 해요.
[seolssareul haeyo]

● I have indigestion.
소화가 안 돼요.
[sowhaga an dwaeoyo]

● I've been sick since yesterday.
어제부터 아팠어요.
[eojebuteo apasseoyo]

● I have a cold. (= I catch a cold.)
감기에 걸렸어요.
[gamgi-e geolryeosseoyo]

● I have a stuffy nose.
코가 막혀요.
[koga makyeoyo]

● I have a runny nose.
콧물이 나요.
[konmuri nayo]

● I can't hear well.
잘 안들려요.
[jal an deulryeoyo]

- **I have a soar throat.**
  목구멍이 아파요.
  [mokkumeongi apayo]

- **I ache all over. (= I have a bodyache.)**
  온 몸이 아파요.
  [on momi apayo]

- **I'm pregnant.**
  임신 중이에요.
  [imsin jung-i-eyo]

- **I have an allergy to(certain) medication.**
  약 알레르기가 있어요.
  [yak allereugiga isseoyo]

- **I have high blood pressure.**
  고혈압이 있어요.
  [gohyeorabi isseoyo]

- **I have diabetes.**
  당뇨병이 있어요.
  [dangnyobyeongi isseoyo]

- **I am having chest pains.**
  가슴이 아파요.
  [gaseumi apayo]

- **It is hard to take a breath.**
  숨쉴 때 힘들어요.
  [sumshil ttae himdeureoyo]

● **I have pain in my ankles.**
발목이 아파요.
[balmogi apayo]

● **My shoulders are sore.**
어깨가 아파요.
[eokkaega apayo]

● **I am constipated.**
변비가 심해요.
[byeonbiga simhaeyo]

● **My body is itchy.**
몸이 가렵습니다.
[momi garyeopsseumnida]

● **I have to urinate too often.**
소변을 자주 봅니다.
[sobyeneul jaju bomnida]

● **It's painful when I urinate.**
소변 볼 때 아파요.
[sobyeon bol ttae apayo]

● **I hurt my back.**
허리를 다쳤어요.
[heolireul dachyeosseoyo]

● **How long does it take to be recovered?**
(= When do I expect to be fully recovered?)
언제쯤 나을까요?
[eonjejjeum na-eulkkayo]

● **I have a toothache.**

이가 아픕니다.

[iga apeumnida]

● **Can you introduce to me a good dental clinic?**

치과 좀 소개 시켜 주시겠습니까?

[chigwa jom sogae sikyeo jusigesseumnikka]

● **I have cavities.**

충치가 생겼어요.

[chungchiga saenggyeosseoyo]

● **How may I help you? (= What's the problem?)**

무슨 문제입니까?

[museun munje-imnikka]

● **How much does it cost?**

비용은 얼마나 듭니까?

[biyongeum eolmana deumnikka]

● **Does the insurance cover it?**

보험은 됩니까?

[boheomeun doemnikka]

● **How long does it take to get treated?**

치료 기간이 얼마나 걸릴까요?

[chiryo gigani eolmana geolrilkkayo]

● **Please, be careful. I'm very sensitive.**

아프지 않게 해 주세요.

[apeuji anke hae juseyo]

- **When am I supposed to come again?**

또 언제 와야 합니까?

[tto eonje waya hamnikka]

- **Can I reschedule for another day?**

다른 날로 예약을 정했으면 좋겠습니다.

[dareun nalro yeyageul jeonghaesseumyeon jokesseumnida]

- **Do you take credit cards?**

카드로 계산이 됩니까?

[kadeuro gyesani doemnikka]

At a Pharmacy (Drugstore) 약국에서 yakkuk-eseo

- **Can I get some cold medicine?**

감기약 있어요?

[gamgiyak isseoyo]

- **Can I have some cough medicine?**

기침약 주세요.

[gichimyak juseyo]

- **I need an asprin(painrelifer) for my headache.**

두통약 주세요.

[dutongyak juseyo]

- **My stomach is upset. Can I have some medicine?**

배탈약 주세요.

[baetalryak juseyo]

- **Can I have a stool softner pill? (= Can I have a laxative.)**

변비약 주세요.

[byeonbiyak juseyo]

● **I need plaster tape, please.**
반창고 주세요.
[banchanggo juseyo]

● **I need some vitamins, please.**
비타민 주세요.
[bitamin juseyo]

● **I need some contraception pills.**
피임약 주세요.
[pi-imyak juseyo]

● **I am looking for some iron supplements.**
철분제 주세요.
[cheolbunje juseyo]

● **Can I have some nutritional supplements?**
영양제 주세요.
[yeongyangje juseyo]

● **Bandage, please.**
밴드 주세요.
[baendeu juseyo]

● **I need some hemostatic.**
지혈제 주세요.
[jihyeoljje juseyo]

● **Can I have some ointment?**
연고 주세요.
[yeongo juseyo]

- **Here is your prescription.**
  처방전 여기 있어요.
  [cheobangjeon yeogi isseoyo]

- **How much is it for the medicine?**
  약 값이 얼마입니까?
  [yak gabsi eolmaimnikka]

10 Transportation | 교통수단 이용　*gyotongsudan iyong*

Rent

- **I'd like to rent a car, please?**
  차를 렌트하고 싶습니다.
  [chareul lenteuhago sipsseumnida]

- **Do you have an international driver's licence?**
  국제 운전면허증을 가지고 있습니까?
  [gukjje unjeon myeonheojjeungeul gajigo isseumnikka]

- **How much is it for a 2day-rental?**
  이틀을 렌트하는 데 얼마입니까?
  [iteureul lenteuhaneun de eolma-imnikka]

Bus

- **Where is the bus stop?**
  버스 정류장은 어디입니까?
  [beoseu jeongnyujangeun eodi-imnikka]

- **Take a turn left and go straight for about 5 minutes.**

  왼쪽으로 돌아가서 5분 쯤 걸으면 돼요.

  [oenjjogeuro doragaseo obun jjeum georeumyeon dwaeyo]

- **Where can I buy a T-money card?**

  어디에서 교통카드를 살 수 있나요?

  [eodi-eseo gyotong kadeureul sal su innayo]

- **The right booth over there.**

  저 쪽 오른쪽 부스예요.

  [jeo jjok oreunjjok buseuyeyo]

- **How much is it for a T- card?**

  교통카드는 얼마예요?

  [gyotong kadeuneun eolmayeyo]

- **How much is the airport limousine bus fare?**

  공항 리무진 버스 요금이 얼마입니까?

  [gonghang limujin beoseu yogeumi eolma-imnikka]

- **What buses go to a city hall?**

  시청으로 가는 버스는 몇 번입니까?

  [sicheong-euro ganeun beoseuneun myeotppeonimnikka]

- **How much is the bus fare?**

  요금이 얼마입니까?

  [yogeumi eolma imnikka]

- **Do you take credit cards?**

  카드도 되나요?

  [kadeudo doenayo]

- **How many stops left to a city hall?**
시청까지 몇 정거장을 더 가야 하나요?
[sicheongkkaji myeot jeonggeojangeul deo gaya hanayo]

- **How long will it take?**
얼마나 걸립니까?
[eolmana geolrimnikka]

- **Where (=Which bus stop) should I get off?**
어디에서 내려야 좋을까요?
[eodi-e-seo naeryeoya joeulkkayo]

- **Please, drop me off here.**
여기에서 내리겠습니다.
[yeogi-e-seo naerigesseumnida]

Subway

- **Where is the closest subway station?**
가까운 지하철 역은 어디 있나요?
[gakkaun jihacheol yeogeun eodi innayo]

- **Take subway line number 2.**
지하철 2 호선을 타세요.
[jihacheol i hoseoneul taseyo]

- **What subway lines do I have to take to Angukdong?**
안국동을 가려면 몇 호선을 타야 합니까?
[anguktongeul garyeomyeon myeot hoseoneul taya hamnikka]

- **Can I have a subway map, please?**
지하철 노선표를 주세요.

[jihacheol noseonpyoleul juseyo]

● **Which exit do I have to take to go to Gyeongbokgoong?**
경복궁을 가려면 어느 출구로 나가야 합니까?
[KYEONGBOKGUNGeul garyeomyeon eoneu chulguro nagaya-
  hamnikka]

● **Can I have one ticket, please?**
표 한 장 주세요.
[pyo han jang juseyo]

● **Which way do I take to board?**
어느 쪽에서 타야 합니까?
[eoneu jjogeseo taya hamnikka]

● **Which way to transfer to line #1?**
1 호선으로 갈아타려면 어느 쪽으로 가야 합니까?
[il hoseoneuro garataryeomyeon eoneujjogeuro gaya hamnikka]

Taxi

● **Where is the taxi stand?**
택시 정류장이 어디 입니까?
[taekssi jeongnyujangi eodi imnikka]

● **Can you go to Seoul station?**
서울역으로 가 주세요.
[Seoulyeogeuro ga juseyo]

● **How long does it take by taxi?**
택시로 얼마나 걸립니까?
[taekssiro eolmana geolrimnikka]

- **It takes about 20 minutes.**
약 20분 가량 걸립니다.
[yak isippun garyang geolrimnida]

- **Please, close the window.**
창문을 닫아주세요.
[changmuneul dadajuseyo]

- **Please, move slowly.**
천천히 가 주세요.
[cheoncheoni ga juseyo]

- **Can you take me to Hotel Lotte?**
롯데호텔로 가 주세요.
[Lotte hotelro ga juseyo]

- **How long does it take to the airport?**
공항까지 시간이 얼마나 걸립니까?
[gonghangkkaji sigani eolmana geolrimnikka]

- **How much is the fare to the airport?**
공항까지 요금이 얼마입니까?
[gonghangkkaji yogeumi eolma-imnikka]

- **Let me get off here.**
여기 내려 주세요.
[yeogi naeryeo juseyo]

- **Keep the change.**
잔돈은 가지세요.
[jandoneun gajiseyo]

Where can I buy the train ticket?

기차표를 사려면 어디에서 사야합니까?

[gichapyoreul saryeomyeon eodi-e-seo sayahamnikka]

Which exit do I have to take to the train platform?

기차를 타려면 어느 출구로 나가야 하나요?

[gichareul taryeomyeon eoneu chulguro nagaya hanayo]

How long does it take to Daejeon by KTX?

대전까지 KTX로 가면 시간이 얼마나 걸립니까?

[daejeon kkaji KTXro gamyeon sigani eolmana geolrimnikka]

Can I have one KTX ticket for DaeJeon?

대전 행 KTX 표 한 장 주세요.

[daejeon haeng KTX pyo han jang juseyo]

One ticket to Busan, please.

부산 행으로 한 장 주십시오.

[busan haengeuro han jang jusipsiyo]

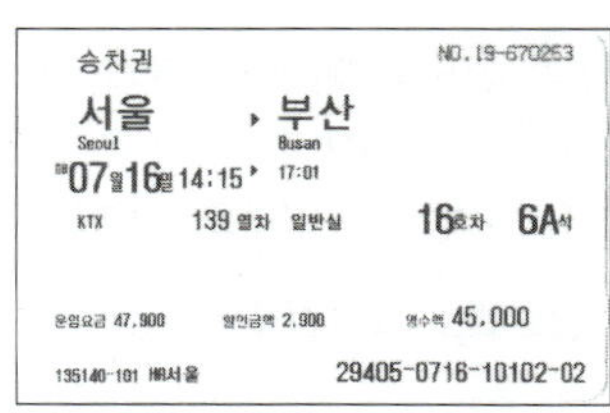

〈KTX Boarding Pass〉

Do you have any cheaper fare rates?

좀 더 싼 표도 있습니까?

[jom deo ssan pyodo isseumnikka]

Sorry, this seat is taken. (= Here is my seat)

여기는 제 자리입니다.

[yeogineun je jari-imnida]

Where is a dining car?

식당 칸은 어디입니까?

[siktang kaneun eodi-imnikka]

● **The business hour of this post office is from 9a.m. to 6p.m. on Mondays through to Fridays.**

우체국은 월요일–금요일 오전 9시부터 오후 6시까지 이용할 수 있습니다.

[ucheguegeun woryoil - geumyoil ojeonbuteo ohu yeoseotssikkaji iyong hal su isseumnida]

● **This post office serves with general domestic mail services including shipping, handling and banking services.**

우체국에서는 국내 외 우편 업무, 택배, 예금 등을 다룹니다.

[uchegugeseoneun gungnae oe upyeon eommu, taekppae, yegeum deungeul darumnida]

● **May I send this parcel to U.S.?**

이 소포를 미국으로 보내려고 합니다.

[i soporeul migugeuro bonaeryeogo hamnida]

● **What's in it?**

내용물이 무엇입니까?

[naeyongmuri mueosimnikka]

● **They are clothes and a pair of shoes.**

옷과 구두입니다.

[otkwa gudu-imnida]

● **Would you put them in the box and place on the scale, please?**

상자에 넣어서 저울에 올려 주세요.

[sangja-e neo-eoseo jeoure olryeo juseyo]

● **How much is it?**

요금이 얼마입니까?

[yogeumi eolma-imnikka]

● **How long does it take via regular air?**
일반 항공편은 얼마나 걸립니까?
[ilban hanggongpyeoneun eolmana geolrimnikka]

● **It will take about a week.**
일주일 정도 걸립니다.
[iljju-il jeongdo geolrimnida]

● **Can I send it by EMS?**
EMS(특급우편)로 보내겠습니다.
[EMS(teukkeup upyeon)ro bonaegesseumnida]

● **It comes out__________. Do you need a receipt?**
__________입니다. 영수증 드릴까요?
[__________ imnida. Yeongsujeung deurikkayo]

12 **On the street | 길거리에서** *gilkkeori-eseo*

● **Can you help me, please?**
도와 주시겠어요?
[dowa jusigesseoyo]

● **How may I help you?**
무엇을 도와 드릴까요?
[mueoseul dowa deurikkayo]

● **Where is the bus station?**
버스 정거장이 어디입니까?
[beoseu jeonggeojangi eodi-imnikka]

- **Turn on the right and it's on the corner.**
오른쪽으로 돌아가서 모퉁이에 있습니다.
[oreunjjogeuro doragaseo motung-ie isseumnida]

- **How far is it from here?**
여기서 얼마나 멉니까?
[yeogiseo eolmana meomnikka]

- **It is nearby. (= It's close.)**
가까이에 있습니다.
[gakka-ie isseumnida]

- **How long will it take?
(=) How long does it take?**
얼마나 걸립니까?
[eolmana geolrimnikka]

- **It will take about 10 minutes on foot.**
걸어서 10분 정도 걸립니다.
[georeoseo sippun jeogdo geolrimnida]

- **I'm looking for a city hall, please?**
시청을 찾고 있습니다.
[sicheongeul chakko isseumnida]

- **I am going in the same direction.**
저도 같은 방향으로 갑니다.
[jeodo gateun bahyangeuro gamnida]

- **How can I find out?**
어떻게 찾을 수 있을까요?
[eotteoke chajeul su isseulkkayo]

- **You can easily find it. (= You can't miss it!)**
쉽게 찾을 수 있습니다.
[swipkke chajeul su isseumnida]

- **I'm going to ______, please.**
~로 가 주세요.
[~ro ga juseyo]

- **How much is the fare?**
요금이 얼마입니까?
[yogeumi eolma-imnikka]

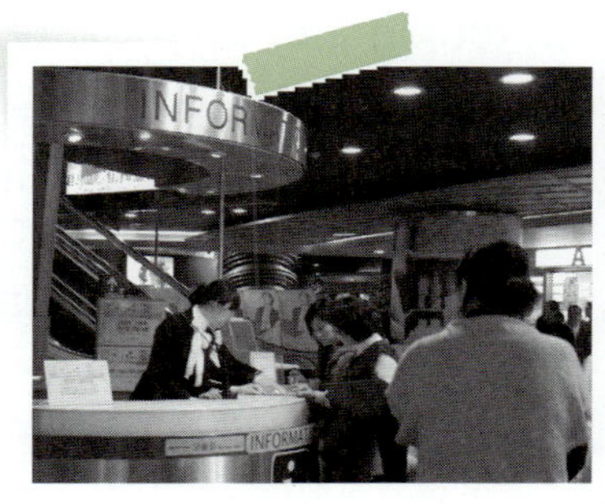

- **Can I go on foot?**
걸어서 갈 수 있나요?
[georeoseo gal su innayo]

- **No, you'd better take the bus.**
아니요, 버스를 타야 합니다.
[aniyo, beoseureul taya hamnida]

13 On a trip / travel / get away | 여행지에서 yeohaengji-eseo

- **Is any hotel around here?**
이 근처에 호텔이 어디 있나요?
[i geuncheo-e hoteri eodi innnayo]

- **Where are the restrooms?**
화장실이 어디인가요?
[hwajangsiri eodiingayo]

- **How do I get there?**

어떤 교통을 이용하면 좋을까요?
[eotteon gyotongeul iyonghamyeon jo-eulkkayo]

- **I'm looking for an inexpensive accomodation.**

싼 모텔을 이용하고 싶습니다.
[ssan motereul iyonghago sipsseumnida]

- **How do I use the rental car service?**

렌터카를 이용하고 싶습니다.
[lenteokareul iyonghago sipsseumnida]

- **Where is a convenient store?**

편의점은 어디에 있나요?
[pyeonuijeomeun eodi-e innayo]

- **Where can I find some famous attractions?**

유명한 관광지는 어디인가요?
[yumyeonghan gwangwangjineun eodi-ingayo]

- **Where is a post office?**

우체국은 어디에 있나요?
[uchegugeun eodi-e innayo]

- **Where is stationery store?**

문구점은 어디에 있나요?
[mungujeomeun eodi-e innayo]

- **Can I drink this water? (= Is this water drinkable?)**

이 물을 마셔도 되나요?
[i mureul masyeodo doenayo]

Taking a walk with Korean

한국어로 산책하기

hangugeoro sanchaekagi

Section 01 | A-Z Vocabulary of English 영어 어휘 yeong-eo eohwi A-Z

Section 02 | ㄱ-ㅎ Vocabulary Collection 한국어 어휘 hangugeo eohwi ㄱ-ㅎ

영어 어휘

yeong-eo eohwi A-Z

A (indefinite article)

● **Accident** 사고 [sago]

There is a car accident.

차 사고가 났습니다.

[cha sagoga nasseumnida]

● **Account** 계좌 [gyejwa]

Tell me your bank account number.

당신의 계좌 번호를 말해 주세요.

[dansinui gyejwa beonhoreul marae juseyo]

● **Actor (male)** 남자 배우 [namja bae-u]

He is an actor.

그는 배우입니다.

[geuneun bae-u-imnida]

● **Actress (female)** 여자 배우 [yeoja bae-u]

She is an actress.

그녀는 배우입니다.

[geunyeoneun bae-u-imnida]

● **Address** 주소 [juso]

May I have your address, please?

주소가 어떻게 됩니까?

[jusoga eotteoke doemnikka]

- **Adult** 어른 [eoreun]

  I want to be an adult.

  어른이 되고 싶어요.

  [eoreuni doego sipeoyo]

- **Advertise** 광고하다 [gwanggohada]

  He advertised for help.

  그는 구인 광고를 냈습니다.

  [geuneun gu-in gwangoreul naesseumnida]

- **Advice** 충고, 조언 [chunggo, jo-eun]

  Please, give me a piece of advice.

  조언 부탁 드려요.

  [jo-eon butak deureoyo]

- **After** 후에, 다음에, 뒤에 [hu-e, da-eume, dwi-e]

  After 10 minutes.

  십 분 후에

  [sip bun hu-e]

- **Afternoon** 오후 [ohu]

  What are you doing this afternoon?

  오후에는 뭘 하세요?

  [ohu-eneun mwol haseyo]

- **Again** 다시, 또 [dasi ,tto]

  I'll see you again.

  다시(또) 뵙겠습니다.

  [dasi(tto) boepgesseumnida]

- **Age** 연세, 나이 [yeon-se, na-i]

  How old are you?(=How old are you?)

  나이가 어떻게 되세요?

  [na-iga eotteoke doeseyo]

- **Agency** 대리점 [daerijeom]

  It's a travel agency.

  그곳은 여행사입니다.

  [geugoseun yeohaengsa-imnida]

- **Agreement** 동의 [dong-ui]

  We had an agreement. (= We all agree.)

  우리는 동의했습니다.

  [urineun dong-uihaessseumnida]

- **Air** 공기 [gonggi]

  The air is really fresh.

  공기가 참 신선하군요.

  [gongiga cham sinseonhagunyo]

- **Airline** 항공 [hanggong]

  What airline do you fly with?

  어떤 항공을 이용하세요?

  [eotteon hangongeul iyonghaseyo]

- **Airplane** 비행기 [bihaenggi]

  The airplane is taking off now.

  비행기가 지금 이륙합니다.

  [bihaenggiga jigeum iryukamnida]

- **Airport** 공항 [gonghang]

  What time do you want to meet at the airport?

  공항에서 몇 시에 만날까요?

  [gonghangeseo myeot ssie manalkkayo]

- **Airport terminal** 공항 터미널 [gonghangteominal]

  Where is the airport terminal?

  공항 터미널이 어디입니까?

  [gonghang teomineori eodi imnikka]

- **Alarm** 알람 [alram]

  There was a fire alarm.

  소방 알람이 울렸습니다.

  [sobang alrami ulryeosseumnida]

- **Alcohol** 알코올 [alcol]

  Alcohol needs to be handled with care.

  알코올은 조심해서 다루어야 합니다.

  [alco-oreun josimhaeseo daru-eoya hamnida]

- **All** 모두, 모든 [modu, modeun]

  You can see all the things here.

  여기에 모든 것이 있습니다.

  [yeogi-e modeun geosi isseumnida]

- **Allergy** 알레르기 [allereugi]

  I have an allergy to peaches.

  나는 복숭아 알레르기가 있어요.

  [naneun boksung-a alrereugiga isseoyo]

● **Almost** 거의 [geo-ui]

I am almost done.

거의 다 했어요.

[geo-ui da haesseoyo]

● **Alphabet** 알파벳 [alpabet]

Do you know the English alphabets?

당신은 영어 알파벳을 아십니까?

[dangsineun yeong-eo alpabeseul asimnikka]

● **Already** 이미 [imi]

I've already finished.

나는 이미 끝냈습니다.

[naneun imi kkeunnaesseumnida]

● **Also** 역시, 또한 [yeokssi, ttohan]

I also think that way.

나도 역시(또한) 그렇게 생각합니다.

[nado yeokssi geureoke saengakamnida]

● **America** 미국 [migug]

There are 50 states in America.

미국은 50개 주입니다.

[migugeun osipgae ju-imnida]

● **Amusement park** 놀이 공원 [norigongwon]

Amusement parks are fun.

놀이 공원은 재미있습니다.

[norigongwoneun jaemi isseumnida]

- **Animal** 동물 [dongmul]

There are a lot of animals at a zoo.

동물원에는 동물이 많습니다.

[dongmurwoneneun dongmuri mansseumnida]

- **Anniversary** 기념일 [ginyeomil]

Today is the 15th wedding anniversary .

오늘은 결혼 15주년 기념일입니다.

[oneureun gyeoron sibojunyeon ginyeomilimnida]

- **Announcement** 공고, 발표 [gong go balpyo]

There was an ______ announcement today .

오늘 ______을 발표했습니다.

[oneul ______ eul balpyo haesseumnida]

- **Annual** 연례의 [yeon rye (yeolrye)]

The company has an annual meeting.

그 회사는 연례 회의를 합니다.

[geu hoesaneun yeolrye hoe-uireul hamnida]

- **Answer** 대답 [daedap]

Answer me, please.

대답해 주세요.

[daedape juseyo]

- **Apartment** 아파트 [apat]

There are many apartments in Korea.

한국에는 아파트가 많습니다.

[hangugeneun apateuga mansseumnida]

- **Apologize** 사과하다 [sagwahada]

  I apologize to you.

  당신에게 사과 드릴게요.

  [dangsinege sagwa deurilkkeyo]

- **Apple** 사과 [sagwa]

  Apples are yummy.

  사과는 맛있습니다.

  [sagwaneun masisseumnida]

- **Area** 지역,구역 [jiyeok, guyeok]

  This is a non-smoking area.

  여기는 금연 구역입니다.

  [yeogineun geumyeon guyeogimnida]

- **Arrival** 도착 [dochak]

  When is the arrival time?

  도착 시간이 언제입니까?

  [dochak sigani eonjeimnika]

- **Artist** 예술가 [yesulga]

  I want to be an artist.

  나는 예술가가 되고 싶어요.

  [naneun yesulgaga doego sipeoyo]

- **Asia** 아시아 [asia]

  Have you ever been in Asia?

  아시아에 가 본 적이 있습니까?

  [asia-e ga bon jeogi isseumnikka]

● **Assistance** 조력자 [joryeokja]

Find the assistance.

조력자를 찾으세요.

[joryeokjjareul chajeuseyo]

● **Association** 협회 [hyeophoi]

There are many trade associations.

많은 무역 협회가 있습니다.

[maneun muyeok hyeopoega isseumnida]

● **Athlete** 운동 선수 [undong seonsu]

My uncle is an athlete.

삼촌은 운동 선수입니다.

[samchoneun undong seonsu-imnida]

● **Audience** 청중 [cheongjung]

The audience applauds.

청중들은 기립박수를 보냈습니다.

[cheongjungdeureun girippaksureul bonaesseumnida]

● **Audio** 오디오 [odio]

You can listen to the music with audio.

당신은 오디오에서 음악을 들을 수 있습니다.

[dangsineun odio-eseo eumageul deureul su isseumnida]

● **August** 팔월 [parwol]

August in Korea is summer.

한국에서 팔월은 여름입니다.

[hangugeseo parworeun yeoreumimnida]

- **Australia** 오스트레일리아, 호주 [oseuteureilia, hoju]

  There are many kangaroos in Australia.

  호주에는 캥거루가 많습니다.

  [hojueneun kaengeoruga mansseumnida]

- **Author** 작가 [jakkga]

  He is a good author.

  그 작가는 글을 잘 씁니다.

  [geu jakkaneun geureul jal sseumnida]

- **Automobile** 자동차 [jadongcha]

  What kinds of automobile do you like?

  어떤 차를 좋아하세요?

  [etteon chareul joahaseyo]

- **Autumn** 가을 [gaeul]

  Autumn comes.

  가을이 왔습니다.

  [ga-euri wasseumnida]

- **Award** 상 [sang]

  I got an award.

  나는 상을 받았습니다.

  [naneun sangeul badasseumnida]

B

- **Baby sitter** 아기 돌보미 [agi dolbomi]

  That baby sitter loves the baby.

  아기 돌보미는 아기를 사랑합니다.

  [agi dolbomineun agireul saranghamnida]

● **Bad** 나쁜 [nabbeun]

That is such a bad word.

그건 나쁜 말이야.

[geugeon nappeun mariya]

● **Bag** 가방 [gabang]

My bag is big.

내 가방은 큽니다.

[nae gabangeun keumnida]

● **Ball** 공 [bol]

A ball is on the sofa.

소파 위에 공이 있습니다.

[sopawi-e gong-i isseumnida]

● **Banana** 바나나 [banana]

Bananas are long.

바나나는 길어요.

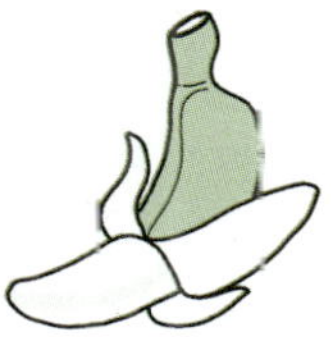

[banananeun gireoyo]

● **Bandage** 반창고 [banchango]

I put a bandage on the scratch.

상처에 반창고를 붙였습니다.

[sangcheo-e banchangoreul buchyeosseumn

● **Bank** 은행 [eunhaeng]

Where can I find the bank?

은행이 어디입니까?

[eunhaeng-i eodi-imnikka]

- **Banquet** 연회 [yeonhoe]

  The banquet was great.

  그 연회는 참 훌륭했습니다.

  [geu yeonhoeneun cham hulryunghaesseumnida]

- **Bar** 바 [ppa]

  I often go to bars on Fridays.

  나는 금요일에 바에 자주 갑니다.

  [naneun geumyoire ppa-e jaju gamnida]

- **Barber shop** 이발소 [ibalso]

  Time to go to the barber shop.

  이발소 갈 때가 되었어요.

  [ibalso gal ttaega doe-eosseoyo]

- **Baseball** 야구 [yagu]

  Let's play baseball game.

  야구 놀이 할까요?

  [yagu nori halkkayo]

- **Basement** 지하 [jiha]

  I don't like the basement.

  나는 지하가 싫어요.

  [naneun jihaga sireoyo]

- **Basketball** 농구 [nonggu]

  Basketball players are tall.

  농구 선수는 키가 큽니다.

  [nonggu seonsuneun kiga keumnida]

- **Bath** 목욕 [mogyok]
  How often do you take a bath?
  얼마나 자주 목욕을 하십니까?
  [eolmana jaju mogyogeul hasimnikka]

- **Bathroom** 욕실, 화장실 [yoksil, whajangsil]
  The bathroom is on the corner.
  화장실은 모퉁이에 있습니다.
  [hwajangsireun motungi-e isseumnida]

- **Battery** 배터리 [baeteori]
  My cellular phone battery is out.
  내 휴대폰 배터리가 나갔어요.
  [nae hyudaepon baeteoriga nagasseoyo]

- **Bay** 만, 항구 [man, hang gu]
  The bay is beautiful.
  항구가 아름답습니다.
  [hangguga areumdapseumnida]

- **Be (present tense)**
  informal present tense : 이다 [ida]
  polite present tense : 입니다 [imnida]
  past tense : 있었습니다 [isseosseumnida]

- **Beach** 해변 [haebyeon]
  Do you like to go to the beach?
  해변을 좋아하세요?
  [haebyeoneul joahaseyo]

● **Bean** 콩 [kong]

Tofu is made of beans.

두부는 콩으로 만들었습니다.

[dubuneun kongeuro mandeureosseumnida]

● **Bear** 곰 [gom]

The bear is strong.

곰은 힘이 셉니다.

[gomeun himi semnida]

● **Beautiful** 아름다운 [areumdaun]

The flowers are beautiful.

꽃은 아름답습니다.

[kkocheun areumdapseumnida]

● **Beauty shop** 미용실 [miyongsil]

I got perm at the beauty shop.

미용실에서 파마를 했습니다.

[miyongsireseo pamareul haesseumnida]

● **Bed** 침대, 잠자리 [chimdae, jamjjari]

When is your bedtime? (= What time do you go to bed?)

언제 잠자리에 듭니까?

[eonje jamjjari-e deumnikka]

● **Bedroom** 침실 [chimsil]

I have to clean up the bedroom.

침실 청소를 해야 합니다.

[chimsil cheongsoreul haeya hamnida]

- **Beef** 소고기 [sogogi]

  Is beef OK with you?

  소고기 어떠세요?

  [sogogi eotteoseyo]

- **Beer** 맥주 [maekjju]

  Would you like a glass of beer?

  맥주 한 잔 하시겠어요?

  [maekjju han jan hasigesseoyo]

- **Before** 전에 [jeone]

  Have we met before?

  우리 전에 만났지요?

  [uri jeone mannajjiyo]

- **Begin** 시작하다 [sijakada]

  We begin to write.

  쓰기 시작했습니다.

  [sseungi sijakaesseumnida]

- **Beginner's class** 초급반 [chogeupban]

  I'm in a beginner's Korean class.

  한국어 초급반입니다.

  [hangugeo chogeuppanimnida]

- **Bellboy** 벨보이 [belboi]

  A bellboy takes the baggage.

  벨보이가 짐을 들어 주었습니다.

  [belboiga jimeul deureo ju-eosseumnida]

Below 아래 [arae]

It's a below the average score.

평균 점수보다 아래입니다.

[pyeongyun jeomsuboda arae-imnida]

Best 최고 [choego]

You are the best!

당신이 최고입니다!

[dangsini choego-imnida]

Better 더 나은 [deonaeun]

Can you show me the better one?

더 나은 것으로 보여주시겠어요?

[deo na-eun geoseuro boyeojusigesseoyo]

Between 사이 [sai]

Between you and I

당신과 나 사이

[dangsingwa na sai]

Bicycle 자전거 [jajeongeo]

I have an old bicycle.

나는 낡은 자전거가 있습니다.

[naneun nalgeun jajeon-geoga isseumnida]

Big 큰 [keun]

I prefer big bags.

나는 큰 가방을 좋아합니다.

[naneun keun gabangeul joahamnida]

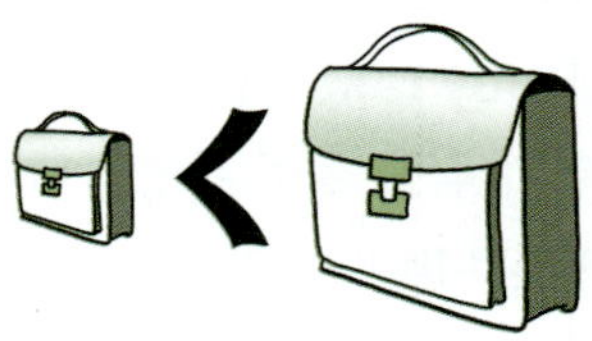

- **Bill** 계산서 [gyesanseo]

Where is the bill?

계산서 어디 있어요?

[gyesanseo eodi isseoyo]

- **Bird** 새 [sae]

A brid flies.

새는 날아 다닙니다.

[saeneun nara danimnida]

- **Birthday** 생일 [saengil]

Today is my birthday.

오늘은 내 생일입니다.

[oneureun nae saeng-i-rimnida]

- **Black** 검은 [geomeun]

Black beans are good for your health.

검은 콩은 몸에 좋아요.

[geomeun kongeun mome joayo]

- **Blanket** 담요 [damnyo]

I need a blanket.

나는 담요가 필요해요.

[naneun damnyoga piryohaeyo]

- **Blond** 금발의 [guembareui]

She has blond hair. (= She is a blond.)

그녀는 금발 머리입니다.

[geunyeoneun geumbal meori-imnida]

● **Blood** 피, 혈액 [pi, hyeoraek]

We need some blood.

우리는 혈액이 필요합니다.
[urineun hyeoraegi piryohamnida]

● **Blood pressure** 혈압 [hyeorap]

How's your blood pressure?

혈압이 어떠세요?
[hyeorabi eotteoseyo]

● **Blue** 파란, 푸른 [paran, pureun]

My car is blue.

내 차는 파란색 입니다.
[nae chaneun paransaegimnida]

● **Boat** 보트 [bot]

I want to have a boat.

나는 보트를 갖고 싶어요.
[naneun boteureul gakko sipeoyo]

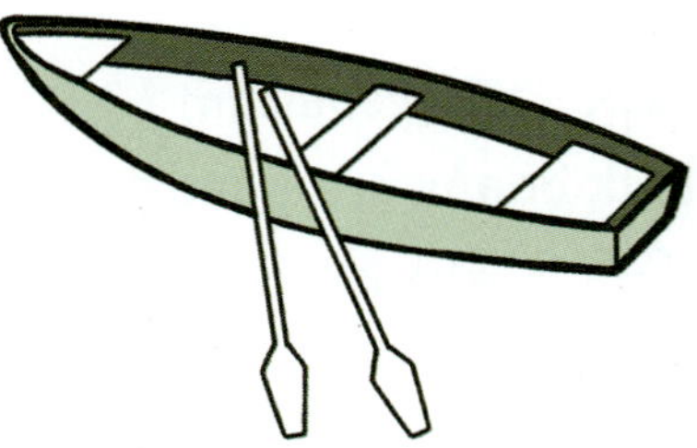

● **Body** 몸, 신체, 인체 [mom, sinche, inche]

The human body is mysterious.

인체는 신비롭습니다.
[incheneun sinbiropsseumnida]

● **Bomb** 폭탄 [poktan]

A bomb is dangerous.

폭탄은 위험합니다.
[poktaneun wiheomhamnida]

- **Bone** 뼈 [ppeyo]

  Bones need calcium.

  뼈는 칼슘을 필요로 합니다.
  [ppyeoneun kalsyumeul piryoro hamnida]

- **Bonus** 보너스 [boneoseu]

  We will get bonues.

  우리는 보너스를 받습니다.
  [urineun boneoseureul basseumnida]

- **Book** 책, 서적 [chaek, seojeok]

  I have lots of books.

  나는 많은 책을 가지고 있습니다.
  [naneun maneun chaegeul gajigo isseumnida]

- **Bookstore** 서점 [seojeom]

  Let's meet at the bookstore.

  서점에서 만나요.
  [seojemeseo mannayo]

- **Booth** 부스 [buseu]

  There are many booths in the exhibition.

  전시회에 많은 부스가 있습니다.
  [jeonsihoe-e maneun buseuga isseumnida]

- **Border** 경계, 국경 [gyeongye, gukyeong]

  Look, there is border!

  저기가 국경입니다.
  [jeogiga gukyoeng-imnida]

● **Born** 태어난 [tae-eonan]

The day you were born is called your birthday.

태어난 날을 생일이라고 합니다.
[tae-eonan nareul saeng-il-irago hamnida]

● **Boss** 상사 [sangsa]

My boss is tough.

나의 상사는 엄합니다.
[nae-ui sangsaneun eomhamnida]

● **Bottle** 병 [byeong]

Two bottles, please.

두 병 주세요.
[du byeong juseyo]

● **Bottom** 바닥 [badak]

You can see the botton.

바닥이 보입니다.
[badagi boimnida]

● **Box** 상자 [sangja]

It's my box.

이것은 나의 상자입니다.
[igeoseun nae-ui sangjaimnida]

● **Boy (son)** 소년, 아들 [sonyeon, adeul]

I have a boy.

나는 아들이 있습니다.
[naneun adeuri isseumnida]

- **Boyfriend** 남자 친구 [namja chingu]

My boyfriend is cute.

나의 남자 친구는 귀엽습니다.

[na-ui namja chinguneun gwiyeobsseumnida]

- **Brain** 뇌 [noi]

The brain is important.

뇌는 중요합니다.

[noeneun jungyohamnida]

- **Branch** 가지, 지점 [gaji jijeom]

There is a short branch on the tree.

짧은 나뭇가지가 있습니다.

[jjalbeun namukkajiga isseumnida]

- **Brand** 상표 [sangpyo]

That is a famous brand.

그것은 유명한 상표입니다.

[geugeoseun yumyeonghan sangpy-oimnida]

- **Bread** 빵 [ppang]

I like bread.

나는 빵을 좋아합니다.

[naneun ppangeul joahamnida]

- **Break (broke)** 깨뜨리다, 헤어지다 [kkaetteurida, heyeojida]

She broke up with her boyfriend.

그녀는 남자 친구와 헤어졌습니다.

[geunyeoneun namja chinguwa heyeojyeosseumnida]

- **Breakfast** 아침 식사 [achim sikssa]

Did you have breakfast?
아침 식사 하셨어요?
[achim sikssa hasyeosseoyo]

- **Bride** 신부 [sinbu]

The bride is happy.
신부는 기뻐합니다.
[sinbuneun gippeohamnida]

- **Bridge** 다리 [dari]

We have to cross the bridge.
다리를 건너야만 합니다.
[darireul geonneoyaman hamnida]

- **Briefcase** 서류 가방 [seoryu gabang]

I buy a briefcase for the birthday gift.
생일 선물로 서류 가방을 샀습니다.
[saengil seonmulro seoryu gabangeul sasseumnida]

- **Britain** 영국 [yeong guk]

Have you ever been to Britain(= England)?
영국에 가 보셨어요?
[yeongguge ga bosyeosseoyo]

- **Brochure** 전단지 [jeondanji]

They make brochures.
그들은 전단지를 만들었습니다.
[geudeureun jeondanjireul mandeureosseumnida]

- **Broker** 중개인 [jung gae-in]

  He is a real estate broker.

  그는 부동산 중개인입니다.

  [geuneun budongsan junggae-in-imnida]

- **Brother** 형제 [hyeongje]

  I have an older brother.

  나는 형이 있습니다.

  [naneun hyeong-i isseumnida]

- **Brown** 갈색 [galsaek]

  The leaves are turning brown.

  나뭇잎이 갈색으로 변했습니다.

  [namunnipi galsaegeuro byeonhaesseumnida]

- **Buddhism** 불교 [bulgyo]

  Buddhism is from India.

  불교는 인도에서 왔습니다.

  [bulgyoneun indo-eseo wasseumnida]

- **Budget** 예산 [yesan]

  We set up the budget for the year.

  우리는 한 해 예산을 짰습니다.

  [urineun han hae yesaneul jjasseumnida]

- **Buffet** 뷔페 [bwipe]

  There are many kinds of food at the buffet.

  뷔페에 가면 많은 음식이 있습니다.

  [bwipe-e gamyeon maneun eumsigi isseumnida]

- **Building** 빌딩, 건물 [bilding geonmul]

  There are a lot of buildings in the city.

  도시에는 빌딩이 많습니다.

  [dosi-eneun bilding-i mansseumnida]

- **Bulgogi** 불고기 [bulgogi]

  Bulgogi is delicious.

  불고기는 맛있어요.

  [bulgogineun masisseoyo]

- **Bus** 버스 [beoseu]

  Where is the bus stop?

  버스 정류장이 어디입니까?

  [beoseu jeongnyujangi eodi-imnikka]

- **Bus stop** 버스 정류장 [beoseu jeong-nyujang]

  The bus stop is close.

  버스 정류장은 가깝습니다.

  [beoseu jeongnyujangeun gakkapsseumnida]

- **Business** 사업 [saeop]

  Does your business go well?

  사업 잘 됩니까?

  [sa-eop jal doemnikka]

- **Business trip** 출장 [chuljang]

  How's your business trip?

  출장은 어떠셨어요?

  [chuljangeun eotteosyeosseoyo]

● **Butter** 버터 [beoteo]

I spread the butter on the bread.

빵에 버터를 발라 먹습니다.

[ppange beoteoreul balra meokssseumnida]

● **Buy** 사다 [sada]

Do you want to buy a necklace?

당신은 목걸이를 사고 싶습니까?

[dangsineun mogeorireul sago sipsseumnikka]

C

● **Cafe** 카페 [kape]

Let's meet at the cafe.

카페에서 만나요.

[kape-eseo mannayo]

● **Cake** 케이크 [keikeu]

Would you like some cake?

케이크 좋아하세요?

[keikeu joahaseyo]

● **Calculator** 계산기 [gyesangi]

Can I borrow your calculator?

계산기 좀 빌려 주세요.

[gyesangi jom bilryeo juseyo]

● **Call** 부르다, 전화하다 [bureuda, jeonhwahada]

Call me.

전화주세요.

[jeonhwa juseyo]

- **Camera** 카메라 [kamera]

Do you have a camera?

카메라 있어요?

[kamera isseoyo]

- **Company** 동료 [dongnyo]

He's a nice company.

그는 좋은 동료입니다.

[geuneun jo-eun dongnyo-imnida]

- **Campus** 캠퍼스 [kaempeoseu]

The campus is gorgeous.

캠퍼스가 아름답군요.

[kaempeoseuga areumdapkkunyo]

- **Canada** 캐나다 [kaenada]

Where is the capital of Canada?

캐나다의 수도는 어디입니까?

[kaenada-ui sudoneun eodi-imnikka]

- **Cancel** 취소 [chwiso]

Let me cancel the appointment.

약속 취소 할게요.

[yaksok chwiso halgeyo]

- **Cancer** 암 [am]

It's important to prevent cancers in its early stages.

암은 예방이 필요합니다.

[ameun yebang-i piryohamnida]

- **Candy** 사탕 [satang]

  She likes candy.

  그녀는 사탕을 좋아합니다.

  [geunyeoneun satangeul joahamnida]

- **Cap** 모자 [moja]

  The cap looks good on you.

  야구 모자가 잘 어울립니다.

  [yagu mojaga jal eo-ulrimnida]

- **Capital** 수도, 자본 [sudo, jabon]

  Seoul is the capital of the Republic of Korea.

  서울은 대한민국의 수도입니다.

  [Seoureun daehanmingug-ui sudo-imnida]

- **Car** 차 [cha]

  What color is your car?

  당신의 차는 무슨 색깔입니까?

  [dangsin-ui chaneun museun saekkarimnikka]

- **Card (= business card)** 명함 [myeongham]

  May I have a business card?

  명함 한 장 주세요.

  [myeongham han jang juseyo]

- **Careful** 조심해! [josimhae]

  Be careful!

  조심하세요!

  [josimhaseyo]

- **Calendar** 달력 [dalryeok]

There are usually 12sheets in a calendar.

달력은 보통 12장입니다.

[dalryeogeun botong yeol du jangimnida]

- **Carpenter** 목수 [moksu]

He is a great carpenter.

그는 훌륭한 목수입니다.

[geuneun huryunghan mokssu-imnida]

- **Carry** ~을 나르다 [~eul nareuda]

I can carry it.

내가 그것을 나를 수 있어요.

[naega geugeoseul nareul su isseoyo]

- **Cash** 현금 [hyeon-geum]

I have some cash.

나는 현금을 가지고 있습니다.

[naneun hyeon-geumeul gajigo isseum

- **Catalogue** 카탈로그 [katallogue]

There are many pictures of items in a catalogue.

카탈로그에 물건 사진이 많습니다.

[katalrogue-e mulgeon sajini manseumnida]

- **Centimeter** 센티미터 [sentimiteo]

What's your height in centimeters?

키가 몇 센티입니까?

[kiga myeot senti-imnikka]

● **Chair** 의자 [uija]

Sit down on a chair.

의자에 앉으세요.

[uija-e anjeuseyo]

● **Charge** 비용 [biyong]

It charges a lot.

비용이 많이 듭니다.

[biyong-i mani deumnida]

● **Charming** 매력적인 [maeryeokjjeogin]

She is charming.

그녀는 매력적입니다.

[geunyeoneun maeryeokjjeogimnida]

● **Cheap** 싼, 값싼 [ssan, gapssan]

Is there anything cheaper?

더 싼 거 있어요?

[deo ssan geo isseoyo]

● **Check** 계산, 확인 [geysan, hwagin]

Can you bring a check, please?

계산해 주세요.

[gyesanhae juseyo]

Can you check again?

확인해 주세요.

[hwaginhae juseyo]

- **Charming** 매력적인 [maeryeokjjeogin]

  She is charming.

  그녀는 매력적입니다.

  [geunyeoneun maeryeokjjeogimnida]

- **Check in at airport** 공항 ; 탑승수속 [tapseung]

  Where can I check in?

  탑승 수속은 어디서 합니까?

  [tapseung susogeun eodiseo hamnikka]

- **Chicken** 닭, 닭고기 [dak, dakkogi]

  Do you want chicken for dinner?

  저녁에 닭고기 어떠세요?

  [jeonyeoge dakkogi eotteoseyo]

- **Child** 아이 [ai]

  Do you like a child?

  아이를 좋아하세요?

  [aireul joahaseyo]

- **Children** 아이들 [aideul]

  Children go to kindergarten.

  아이들이 유치원에 갑니다.

  [aideuri yuchiwone gamnida]

- **China** 중국 [jung guk]

  It's made in China.

  중국산입니다.

  [junggugssan imnida]

- **Chocolate** 초콜릿 [chokolrit]

  I want some chocolate.

  초콜릿을 먹고 싶어요.
  [chokolriseul meogkko sipeoyo]

- **Chopstick** 젓가락 [jeokkarak]

  Chopsticks are comfortable.

  젓가락은 편합니다.
  [jeokkarageun pyeonhamnida]

- **Christmas** 크리스마스 [keurisseumaseu]

  I'm waiting for Christmas.

  나는 크리스마스를 기다립니다.
  [naneun keurisseumaseureul gidarimnida]

- **Church** 교회 [gyohoi]

  I go to church on Sundays.

  일요일에는 교회에 갑니다.
  [iryoireneun gyohoe-e gamnida]

- **Citizen** 시민 [simin]

  The citizens of Seoul like Han River.

  서울 시민은 한강을 사랑합니다.
  [Seoul simineun hangang-eul saranghamnida]

- **City** 도시 [dosi]

  It's a big city.

  큰 도시입니다.
  [keun dosi-imnida]

- **Claim** 요구, 불만 [yogu, bulman]

  I'm here to claim a traffic sign.

  불만이 있어서 왔습니다.

  [bulmani isseoseo wasseumnida]

- **Climate** 기후 [gihu]

  What's the climate in the summer in Korea?

  한국의 여름 기후는 어떻습니까?

  [hangug-ui yeoreum gihuneun eotteosseumnikka]

- **Clinic** 의원 [uiwon]

  The clinic is on the 2nd floor.

  의원은 2층에 있습니다.

  [uiwoneun i cheung-e isseumnida]

- **Clock** 시계 [sigye]

  Do you have a clock?

  시계 있나요?

  [sigye innayo]

- **Close** 가까이, 근처 ,닫다 [gakka-i, geuncheo-e, datta]

  Is a drugstore close to here?

  이 근처에 약국이 있습니까?

  [i geuncheo-e yakkugi issueumnikka]

  Close the door, please.

  문 닫아 주세요.

  [mun dada juseyo]

- **Clothe** 옷 [ot]

  The clothes are beautiful.

  옷이 참 아름다워요.

  [osi cham areumdawoyo]

- **Cloudy** 흐린 [heurin]

  Do you like cloudy days?

  흐린 날 좋아하세요?

  [heurin nal joahaseyo]

- **Coat** 코트 [koteu]

  We need a coat in winter.

  겨울에는 코트가 필요해요.

  [gyeoureneun koteuga piryohaeyo]

- **Coffee** 커피 [keopi]

  I like coffee.

  나는 커피를 좋아합니다.

  [naneun keopireul joahamnida]

- **Coffee shop** 커피숍 [keopishop]

  I am looking for a coffee shop.

  커피숍을 찾고 있습니다.

  [keopishobeul chakko isseumnida]

- **Coke** 코카콜라 [kokakola]

  He likes coke.

  그는 콜라를 좋아합니다.

  [geu neun kolareul joahamnida]

● **Cold** 추운 [chu-un]

It's cold in winter in Korea.

한국의 겨울은 춥습니다.

[hangug-ui gyeoureun chupsseumnida]

● **Comb** 빗 [bit]

I need a comb.

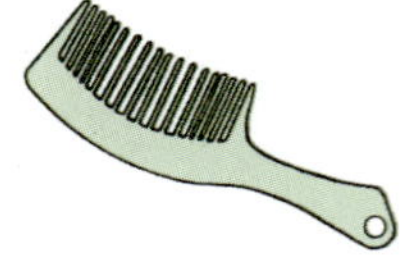

빗이 필요해요.

[bisi piryohaeyo]

● **Come** 오다 [oda]

He's coming.

그는 옵니다.

[geuneun omnida]

● **Communism** 공산주의 [gongsanjueui]

North Korea is a communist country.

북한은 공산주의입니다.

[bukaneun gongsanju-uiimnida]

● **Company** 회사 [hoesa]

It's a big company.

큰 회사입니다.

[keun hoesa-imnida]

● **Competitor** 경쟁자 [gyeongjaengja]

You are my competitor.

당신은 나의 경쟁자입니다.

[dansineun na-ui gyeongjaengja-imnida]

- **Complaint** 불평, 불만 [bulpyeong, bulman]

  I have a complaint for you.(= I have a complaint to make)

  당신에게 불만이 있어요.

  [dansinege bulmani isseoyo]

- **Computer** 컴퓨터 [keomputeo]

  I bought a new computer.

  나는 새 컴퓨터를 샀습니다.

  [naneun sae keomputeoreul sasseumnida]

- **Concert** 콘서트 [konseoteu]

  The concert was great last night.

  어제밤 콘서트는 멋있었어요.

  [eojeppam konseoteuneun meosisseosseoyo]

- **Conductor** 안내자 [an-naeja]

  We need a conductor.

  우리는 안내자가 필요해요.

  [urineun an-naejaga piryohaeyo]

- **Conference** 회의 [hoeui]

  Let's go to the conference room.

  회의실로 갑시다.

  [hoe-uisilro gapsida]

- **Contact lens** 콘택트렌즈 [kontaekteu lenjeu]

  I'm wearing contact lenses.

  나는 콘택트 렌즈를 끼고 있습니다.

  [naneun kontaekteu lenjeureul kkigo isseumnida]

- **Conversation** 대화 [daewha]

We have short conversation.

우리는 짧은 대화를 했습니다.

[urineun jjalbeun daehwareul haesseumnida]

- **Cookies** 쿠키 [kuki]

Do you want some cookies?

쿠키 드시겠어요?

[kuki deusigesseoyo]

- **Cool** 선선한 [seonseonhan]

It's cool in the morning in fall.

가을 아침은 선선합니다.

[ga-eul achimeun seonseonhamnida]

- **Corn** 옥수수 [oksusu]

Boiled corn is tasty.

삶은 옥수수는 맛있어요.

[ssalmeun oksusuneun masisseoyo]

- **Cost (= price)** 가격, 비용 [gagyeok, biyong]

It costs a lot.

비용이 많이 듭니다.

[biyongi mani deumnida]

- **Country** 시골, 나라 [sigol, nara]

I live in the country side.

나는 시골에서 삽니다.

[naneun sigoreseo samnida]

- **Couple** 쌍, 커플 [ssang, keopeul]

That couple is lovely.

저 커플은 잘 어울립니다.

[jeo keopeureun jal eo-ulrimnida]

- **Crab** 게 [ge]

Crab dishes are delicious.

게 요리는 맛있습니다.

[ge yorineun masisseumnida]

- **Cream** 크림 [keurim]

Want some cream with your coffee?

키피에 크림 넣으시겠어요?

[keopi-e keurim neo-eusigesseoyo]

- **Credit card** 신용카드 [sinyongkadeu]

Do you take credit cards?

신용 카드도 됩니까?

[sinyong kadeudo doemnikka]

- **Cup** 컵 [keop]

A cup of water, please.

물 한 컵 주세요.

[mul han keop juseyo]

- **Customer** 손님 [sonnim]

Be kind to customers.

손님에게 친절히!

[sonnimege chinjeori]

- **Cute** 귀여운 [gwiyeoun]

  You are cute.

  당신은 귀엽습니다.

  [dangsineun gwiyeopsseumnida]

D

- **Dad** 아버지 [aboeji]

  My dad is tall .

  아버지는 키가 크십니다.

  [abeojineun kiga keusimnida]

- **Daily** 매일 [mae-il]

  I write journal daily.(= I keep journal everyday)

  나는 매일 일기를 씁니다.

  [naneun mae-il ilgireul sseumnida]

- **Damage** 손상, 피해 [sonsang, pihae]

  The city had damage from the typoon.

  도시는 태풍으로 피해를 입었습니다.

  [dosineun taepung-euro pihaereul ibeosseumnida]

- **Dance** 춤 [chum]

  Shall we dance?

  춤 추실까요?

  [chum chusilkkayo]

- **Dark** 어두운 [eoduun]

  It's dark here.

  여기는 어둡습니다.

  [yeogineun eodupsseumnida]

- **Date** 일 [il]

  What's the date today?

  오늘은 며칠입니까?

  [oneureun myeochilimnikka]

- **Daughter** 딸 [ttal]

  I have a daughter.

  나는 딸이 있습니다.

  [naneun ttari issuemnida]

- **Dawn** 새벽 [saebyeok]

  I wake up before dawn.

  나는 새벽에 일어납니다.

  [naneun saebyeoge ireonamnida]

- **Day** 요일, 날 [yoil, nal]

  What day is it?

  무슨 요일이에요?

  [museun yoirieyo]

- **Delicious** 맛있는 [misineun]

  The food is delicious.

  음식이 맛있습니다.

  [eumsigi masissemnida]

- **Deligent** 부지런한 [bujireonhan]

  Koreans are deligent.

  한국인은 부지런합니다.

  [hangugineun bujireonhamnida]

- **Democracy** 민주주의 [minjujueui]

  The Republic of Korea is a democratic country.

  대한민국은 민주주의 국가입니다.

  [daehanmingugeun minjuju-ui gukka-imnida]

- **Dentist** 치과 의사 [chkgwa uisa]

  He is a dentist.

  그는 치과 의사입니다.

  [geuneun chigwa uisa-imnida]

- **Depart** 출발하다 [chulbalhada]

  I'm departing now.

  지금 출발합니다.

  [jigeum chulbalhamnida]

- **Department store** 백화점 [baekhwajeom]

  I want to go to the department store.

  백화점에 가고 싶어요.

  [baekhwajeome gago sipeoyo]

- **Departure** 출발 [chulbal]

  What's the departure time?

  출발 시간이 언제예요?

  [chulbal sigani eonjeyeyo]

- **Deposit** 예금하다, 저축 [yegeumhada, jeochuk]

  I want to deposit some money.

  나는 저축하고 싶어요.

  [naneun jeochukago sipeoyo]

● **Desert** 사막 [samak]

It's desert.

사막입니다.

[samagimnida]

● **Design** 디자인 [dijain]

Who designed it?

누가 디자인 했나요?

[nuga dijain haennayo]

● **Desk** 책상 [chaeksang]

A book is on the desk.

책상에 책이 있습니다.

[chaesange chaegi isseumnida]

● **Dessert** 후식 [husik]

How's the dessert?

후식 괜찮았어요?

[husik gwaenchanasseoyo]

● **Destination** 목적지 [mokjeokji]

Where is your destination?

목적지가 어디입니까?

[mokjeokjjiga eodi-imnikka]

● **Diamond** 다이아몬드 [daiamondeu]

Diamond is harder than stone.

다이아몬드는 돌보다 강합니다.

[daiamondeuneun dolboda ganghamnida]

- **Dictionary** 사전 [sajeon]

  Look up the dictionary.

  사전을 찾아보세요.

  [sajeoneul chajaboseyo]

- **Diet** 다이어트 [daieoteu]

  You need to go on a diet.

  당신은 다이어트가 필요합니다.

  [dangsineun dai-eoteuga piryohamnida]

- **Difficult** 어렵다, 힘들다 [eoryeopda, himdeulda]

  Korean is not difficult.

  한국어는 어렵지 않습니다.

  [hangugeoneun eoryeopjji anseumnida]

- **Dinner** 저녁식사 [jeonyeoksiksa]

  Do you want to have a dinner together?

  저녁식사 함께 하시겠어요?

  [jeonyeoksiksa hamkke hasigesseoyo]

- **Diploma** 졸업장 [joreopjang]

  I finally got a diploma.

  마침내 졸업장을 받았습니다.

  [machimnae joreopjjangeul badasseumnida]

- **Direct** 직접적인 [jikjeopjeogin]

  I got a direct order from my boss.

  상사에게 직접 명령을 받았습니다.

  [sangsa-ege jikjjeop myeongnyeong-eul badasseumnida]

● **Dirty** 더러운, 지저분한 [deoreoun, jijeobunhan]

Don't touch, that's dirty!

더러워요, 만지지 마세요!

[deoreowoyo manjiji maseyo]

● **Discount** 할인 [harin]

Can you give me a discount?

할인해 주시겠어요?

[harinhae jusigesseoyo]

● **Do** ~을 하다 [~eul hada]

What do you want?

무엇을 하고 싶어요?

[mueoseul hago sipeoyo]

● **Doctor** 의사, 박사 [uisa, baksa]

I'm a doctor.

나는 의사입니다.

[naneun uisa-imnida]

I have a doctor's degree.

나는 박사입니다.

[naneun bakssa-imnida]

● **Dog** 개 [gae]

He is such a big dog!

개가 참 크군요!

[gaega cham keugunyo]

- **Dollar** 달러 [daleo]

  I have a dollar.

  나는 1달러 있어요.

  [naneun il dalreo isseoyo]

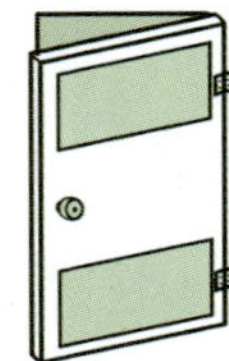

- **Door** 문 [mun]

  Open the door.

  문 여세요

  [mun yeoseyo]

- **Dormitory** 기숙사 [gisuksa]

  Where's your dormitory?

  당신의 기숙사는 어디입니까?

  [dangsinui gisukssaneun eodi-imnikka]

- **Double** 두 배 [du bae]

  It charges double.

  두 배의 비용이 듭니다.

  [du bae-ui biyongi deumnida]

- **Downtown** 시내, 중심가 [sinae, jungsimga]

  Where is downtown?

  시내가 어디입니까?

  [sinaega eodi-imnikka]

- **Dress** 원피스, 옷 [wonpiseu, ot]

  Your dress is pretty.

  원피스가 예뻐요.

  [wonpiseuga yeppeoyo]

● **Drink** 마시다 [masida]

I want to drink some water.

물을 마시고 싶어요.

[mureul masigo sipeoyo]

● **Drive** 운전을 하다 [unjeoneul hada]

Can you drive?

운전 할 줄 아세요?

[unjeon hal jul aseyo]

● **Dry cleaner** 세탁소 [setakso]

Where is a dry cleaner?

세탁소가 어디 있나요?

[setakssoga eodi innayo]

● **During** ～중에 [~junge]

During the meeting

회의 중에

[hoe-ui junge]

● **Dust** 먼지 [meonji]

I hate dust!

먼지가 싫어요.

[meonjiga sireoyo]

● **Duty** 의무 [euimu]

Each citizen has a duty.

국민에게는 의무가 있습니다.

[gungminegeneun uimuga isseumnida]

● **Ear** 귀 [gwi]

My ears are impaired.

귀가 잘 안 들려요.

[gwiga jal an deulryeoyo]

● **Early** 먼저,일찍 [meonjeo, iljjik]

Do you wake up early?(= Are you an early bird?)

일찍 일어납니까?

[iljjik ireonamnikka]

● **East** 동쪽 [dongjjok]

Korea is located in the Far East.

한국은 동쪽 나라입니다.

[hangugeun dongjjok nara-imnida]

● **Easy** 쉬운 [swiun]

It's an easy question.

쉬운 질문입니다.

[swi-un jilmunimnida]

● **Eat** 먹다 [meogtta]

I take vitamin C .

비타민 C를 먹습니다.

[bitamin ssireul meoksseumnida]

● **Economy** 경제 [gyeongje]

The economy has been growing.

경제가 성장했습니다.

[gyeongjega seongjanghaesseumnida]

- **Effort** 노력 [noryeok]

  You will make an effort!

  더 노력하세요.

  [deo noryeokaseyo]

- **Egg** 계란, 달걀 [gyeran, dalgyal]

  One fried egg, please.

  게란 프라이 하나 해 주세요.

  [gyeran peurai hana hae juseyo]

- **Electric** 전기의 [cheongiui]

  This is an Electric company.

  전기 회사입니다.

  [jeongi hoesa-imnida]

- **Elementary school** 초등학교 [chodeunghakkyo]

  An elementary school is close.

  근처에 초등학교가 있습니다.

  [geuncheo-e chodeunghakyoga isseumnida]

- **Elephant** 코끼리 [kokkiri]

  An elephant has a long nose.

  코끼리는 코가 깁니다.

  [kokkirineun koga gimnida]

- **Elevator** 엘리베이터 [elibeiteo]

  The elevator is fast.

  엘리베이터는 빠릅니다.

  [elibeiteoneun ppareumnida]

● **Emergency** 응급, 비상사태 [Eunggeup bisangsatae]

Where is the Emergency Room?

응급실이 어딥니까?

[eunggeupsiri eodi-imnikka]

● **Emigrate** 이민가다 [imingada]

Where do you emigrate to?

어디로 이민 가세요?

[eodiro imin gaseyo]

● **Employee** 종업원 [jongeopwon]

Are you an employee?

종업원이세요?

[jongeobwoniseyo]

● **Enemy** 적 [jeok]

Sleeping with an enemy

적과의 동침

[jeogwa-ui dongchim]

● **Engagement** 약혼 [yakhon (yakon)]

This is an engagement ring.

약혼 반지입니다.

[yakon banji-imnida]

● **England** 영국 [yeongguk]

There is a queen in England.

영국에는 여왕이 있습니다.

[yeonggugeneun yeowangi isseumnida]

● **English** 영어 [yeongeo]
Your English is excellent.
영어를 잘 하시는 군요.
[yeong-eoreul jal hasineungunyo]

● **Enjoy** 즐기다 [jeulgida]
Did you enjoy your weekend?
주말 즐겁게 지내셨어요?
[jumal jeulgeopkke jinaesyeosseoyo]

● **Enough** 충분한 [chungbunhan]
I have enough money.
돈이 충분합니다.
[doni chungbunhamnida]

● **Entrance** 입구 [ipgu]
Come through the entrance.
입구로 들어 오세요.
[ipkkuro deureo oseyo]

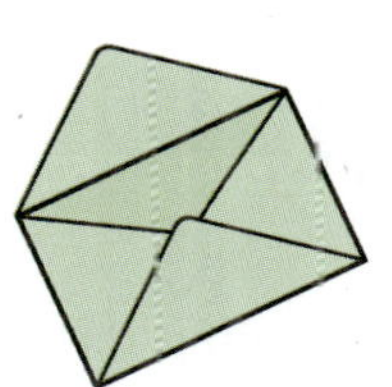

● **Envelope** 봉투 [bongtu]
Give me an envelope.
봉투 한 장 주세요.
[bongtu han jang juseyo]

● **Environment** 환경 [hwangyeong]
Let's protect the environment.
환경을 보호합시다.
[hwangyeongeul bohohapssida]

- **Europe** 유럽 [yureop]

  Do you want to join the tour to Europe?

  유럽 여행 가시겠어요?

  [yureop yeohaeng gasigesseoyo]

- **Evening** 저녁 [jeonyeok]

  See you in the evening!

  저녁에 만나요!

  [jeonyeoge mannayo]

- **Everyday** 날마다 [nalmada]

  I wake up at 7a.m. everyday.

  날마다 7시에 일어납니다.

  [nalmada ilgopsi-e ireonamnida]

- **Excited** 흥분된 [heungbundeon]

  I'm so excited.

  대단히 흥분됩니다.

  [daedani heungbundoemnida]

- **Exercise** 운동 [undong]

  I do exercise every evening.

  매일 저녁 운동을 합니다.

  [mae-il jeonyeok undongeul hamnida]

- **Exit** 출구 [chulgu]

  Go out through the exit.

  출구로 나가세요.

  [chulguro nagaseyo]

- **Expensive** 비싼 [bissan]

Too expensive!

매우 비싸군요!

[mae-u bissagunyo]

- **Express way** 고속도로 [gosokdoro]

We are on the express way.

여기는 고속도로입니다.

[yeogineun gosokdoro-imnida]

- **Eye** 눈 [nun]

Your eyes are beautiful.

눈이 아름답군요.

[nuni areumdapgunyo]

- **Eyebrow** 눈썹 [nunsseop]

Eyebrows are above the eyes.

눈썹은 눈 위에 있습니다.

[nunsseobeun nun wi-e isseumnida]

- **Eyesight** 시력 [siryeok]

I have good eyesight.

눈이 좋습니다.

[nuni josseumnida]

<hr>

F

- **Face** 얼굴 [eolgul]

Your face is pretty.

얼굴이 예쁩니다.

[eolguri yeppeumnida]

● **Factory** 공장 [gongjang]

That is a candy factory.

그 곳은 사탕 공장입니다.

[geu goseun satang gongjang-imnida]

● **Family** 가족 [gajok]

There are 4 in my family.

우리 가족은 네명입니다.

[uri gajogeun ne myeong-imnida]

● **Fan** 부채 [buchae]

Korean fans are pretty.

한국 부채는 예쁩니다.

[hanguk buchaeneun yeppeumnida]

● **Fastfood** 패스트푸드 [paesteupudeu]

Don't go for the fastfood!

패스트푸드를 좋아하지 마세요.

[paeseuteupudeureul joahaji maseyo]

● **Father** 아버지 [abeoji]

My father loves me.

아버지는 나를 사랑하십니다.

[abeojineun nareul saranghasimnida]

● **Female** 여자 [yeoja]

Are you female?

당신은 여자입니까?

[dangsineun yeoja-imnikka]

- **Fever** 열 [yeol]

  He is running a high fever. (= He has a high fever.)

  열이 높아요.

  [yeori nopayo]

- **Fine** 좋은 [joeun]

  It's a fine day.

  좋은 날씨입니다.

  [jo-eun nalssi-imnida]

- **Finger** 손가락 [son garak]

  He has long fingers.

  그는 손가락이 깁니다.

  [geuneun sonkkaragi gimnida]

- **Fingernail** 손톱 [sontop]

  I put polish on my fingernails.

  손톱에 매니큐어를 발랐습니다.

  [sontobe maenikyu-eoreul balrasseumnida]

- **Fire** 불 [bul]

  Be careful with fire!

  불 조심해요!

  [bul josimhae-yo]

- **First** 처음, 먼저 [cheoeum, meonjeo]

  This is my first time.

  처음입니다.

  [cheo-eumimnida]

- **Fish** 생선 [saengseon]

Fish is on season.

생선철입니다.

[saengseoncheorimnida]

- **Floor** 바닥, 층 [badak, cheung]

What floor is it?

몇 층입니까?

[myeot cheungimnikka]

- **Fog** 안개 [angae]

The fog is heavy.

안개가 짙게 끼었습니다.

[angaega jikke kki-eosseumnida]

- **Food** 음식 [eumsik]

What kinds of food do you like?

어떤 음식 좋아하세요?

[eotteon eumsik jo-ahaseyo]

- **Foot** 발 [bal]

My foot is soar.

발이 아픕니다.

[bari apeumnida]

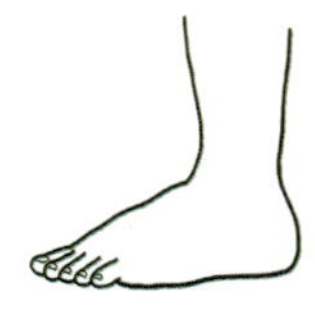

- **Foreigner** 외국인 [oegugin]

There are many foreigners in Itaewon.

이태원에는 외국인이 많습니다.

[itaewoneneun oegugini manseumnida]

● **Fork** 포크 [pokeu]
Give me one more fork.
포크 하나 더 주세요.
[pokeu hana deo juseyo]

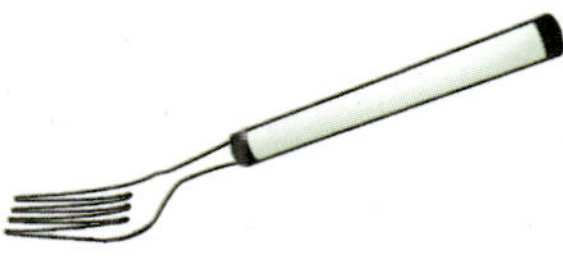

● **France** 프랑스 [peurangseu]
There are many museums in France.
프랑스에는 박물관이 많습니다.
[peurangseueneun bangmulgwani manseumnida]

● **Free** 자유, 무료 [jayu, muryo]
I'm free on the weekends.
주말에 시간 있습니다.
[jumare sigan isseumnida]

It's free.
무료입니다.
[muryo-imnida]

● **Friend** 친구 [chingu]
Do you have many friends?
친구가 많습니까?
[chinguga manseumnikka]

● **From** ~부터, 에서 [~buteo, ~eseo]
From here and there
여기에서 저기에서
[yeogi-eseo jeogi-eseo]

- **Front** 앞에 [ape]

It's in front of you.
당신 앞에 있어요.
[dangsin ape isseoyo]

- **Fruit** 과일 [gwail]

What kind of fruit do you like?
어떤 과일 좋아하세요?
[eotteon gwail joahaseyo]

- **Furniture** 가구 [gagu]

I need change the furniture.
가구를 바꾸어야 합니다.
[gagureul bakku-eoya hamnida]

- **Future** 미래, 장래 [mirae, jangrae]

What do you want to be in the future?
장래 계획이 무엇입니까?
[jangnae gyehwigi mu-eosimnikka]

G

- **Garbage** 쓰레기 [sseuregi]

That's a garbage can.
저기에 쓰레기통이 있습니다.
[jeogi-e sseuregitong-i isseumnida]

- **Garden** 정원 [jeongwon]

Secret Garden
비밀의 정원
[bimirui jeongwon]

- **Garlic** 마늘 [maneul]

We need garlic in Kimchi.

김치에는 마늘이 들어갑니다.

[kimchi-eneun maneuri deureogamnida]

- **Gas station** 주유소 [juyuso]

Is there any gas station?

여기 주유소가 어디입니까?

[yeogi juyosoga eodi-imnikka]

- **Gentleman** 신사답게, 신사 [sinsadapke, sinsa]

You are such a gentleman.

당신은 참 신사답군요.

[dangsineun cham sinsadapkkunyo]

- **Germany** 독일 [dogil]

It's from Germany.

독일산입니다.

[dogilsanimnida]

- **Gift** 선물 [seonmul]

It's my birthday gift.

그것은 생일선물입니다.

[geugeoseun saeng-il seonmurimnida]

- **Ginger** 생강 [saeng gang]

Ginger tea is good for the cold.

생강차는 감기에 좋습니다.

[saenggangchaneun gamgi-e josseumnida]

Ginseng 인삼 [insam]

Korean Ginseng is the best.

한국의 인삼은 최고입니다.

[hangug-ui insameun choego-imnida]

Girl 소녀 [sonyeo]

There are 5 girls.

소녀가 다섯 명 있습니다.

[sonyeoga daseot myeong isseumnida]

Girl friend 여자 친구 [yeoja chingu]

Do you have a girlfriend?

여자 친구가 있습니까?

[yeoja chinguga isseumnika]

Glasses 안경 [angyeong]

I wear eye glasses.

나는 안경을 꼈습니다.

[naneun angyeongeul kkyeosseumnida]

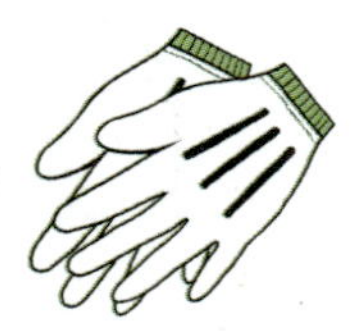

Gloves 장갑 [jang gab]

I need gloves.

나는 장갑이 필요합니다.

[naneun jangabi piryohamnida]

Go 가다 [gada]

I go.

나는 갑니다.

[naneun gamnida]

- **Gold** 금 [geum]

Gold is pricy.

금은 비쌉니다.
[geumeun bissamnida]

- **Good** 좋은 [jo-eun]

Good morning!

좋은 아침!
[jo-eun achim]

- **Graduation** 졸업 [joreop]

Graduation ceremony

졸업식
[joreobssik]

- **Grandchild** 손주 [sonju]

The grandchild is cute.

손주가 귀엽습니다.
[sonjuga gwiyeopsseumnida]

- **Grapes** 포도 [podo]

I like grapes.

나는 포도를 좋아합니다.
[naneun podoreul jo-ahamnida]

- **Green** 녹색 [nokssaek]

The leaves are green.

나뭇잎은 녹색입니다.
[namunipeun nokssaegimnida]

● **Guest** 손님 [sonnim]

A guest comes.

손님이 왔습니다.

[sonnimi wasseumnida]

● **Guide** 안내 [annae]

Guide map

안내도

[annaedo]

● **Gun** 총 [chong]

There was a gun shot.

총소리가 났습니다.

[chongsoriga nasseumnida]

● **Gymnasium** 체육관 [cheyukkwan]

Shall we go to the gymnasium?

체육관에 갈까요?

[cheyukkwane galkkayo]

H

● **Hair** 머리카락 [meorikarag]

A hair dressor trims the hair well.

미용사는 머리를 잘 다듬습니다.

[miyongsaneun meorireul jal dadeumsseumnida]

● **Hand** 손 [son]

Wash your hands.

손 씻으세요.

[son ssiseuseyo]

- **Handbag** 핸드백 [haendeubaek]

  The handbag is very expensive.

  그 핸드백은 매우 비쌉니다.

  [geu haendeubaegeun mae-u bissamnida]

- **Handicapped** 장애인 [jangaein]

  Parking for the handicapped

  여기는 장애인 주차 구역입니다.

  [yeogineun jang-ae-in jucha guyeogimnida]

- **Handmade** 수제품 [sujepum]

  This ring is handmade.

  이 반지는 수제품입니다.

  [i banjineun sujepumimnida]

- **Handsome** 잘생긴 [jalsaenggin]

  You are handsome.

  당신은 잘 생겼습니다.

  [dangsineun jal saengyeosseumnida]

- **Harmony** 조화 [jowha]

  The team works in harmony.

  그 팀은 조화롭습니다.

  [geu timeun johwaropsseumnida]

- **Hat** 모자 [moja]

  Try this hat.

  모자를 써 보세요.

  [mojareul sseo boseyo]

- **Head** 머리 [meori]

  I have a headache.
  머리가 아픕니다.
  [meoriga apeumnida]

- **Health** 건강 [geongang]

  I am taking health supplements.
  나는 건강 식품을 먹고 있습니다.
  [naneun geongang sikpumeul meokko isseumnida]

- **Hear** 듣다 [deutta]

  We hear with our ears.
  귀로 듣습니다.
  [gwiro deusseumnida]

- **Heart** 심장, 마음 [simjang, maeum]

  I'll give my heart.
  내 마음을 드릴게요.
  [nae ma-eumeul deurilkkeyo]

- **Heavy** 무거운 [mugeo-un]

  The book is heavy.
  그 책이 무겁습니다.
  [geu chaegi mugeopsseumnida]

- **Help** 도와주다 [dowajuda]

  Help me, please.
  도와주세요.
  [dowajuseyo]

- **Here** 여기 [yeogi]

  Here and there

  여기저기

  [yeogi jeogi]

- **Highway** 고속도로 [gosokdoro]

  Taking the highway is faster.

  고속도로가 빠릅니다.

  [gosokdoroga ppareumnida]

- **Hill** 언덕 [eondeok]

  It's over the hill.

  언덕 너머에

  [eondeok neomeo-e]

- **History** 역사 [yeoksa]

  Korean history is over 5,000 years old.

  한국의 역사는 오천 년입니다.

  [hangugu-e yeoksaneun ocheon nyeonimnida]

- **Hobby** 취미 [chwimi]

  What's your hobby?

  당신의 취미는 무엇입니까?

  [dangsin-e chwimineun mu-eosimnikka]

- **Holiday** 휴일 [hyuil]

  What do you do during the holidays?

  휴일에는 무얼 하세요?

  [hyu-ireneun mu-eol haseyo]

- **Home** 가정 [gajeong]

Go home.

집으로 가세요.

[jibeuro gaseyo]

- **Hometown** 고향 [gohyang]

We are from the same hometown.

우리는 같은 고향입니다.

[urineun gatteun gohyang-imnida]

- **Honey** 꿀 [kkul]

Honey is sweet.

꿀은 달콤합니다.

[kkureun dalkomhamnida]

- **Honey** 여보 [yeobo]

'Yeobo' is the meaning of 'honey' in Korea.

한국에서는 부부끼리 '여보' 라고 부릅니다.

[hangugeseoneun bubukkiri 'yeobo'rago bureumnida]

- **Hospital** 병원 [byeongwon]

I go to the hospital.

병원에 갑니다.

[byeongwone gamnida]

- **Hot** 뜨거운 [tteugeoun]

Give me some hot tea.

뜨거운 차 한 잔 주세요.

[tteugeoun cha han jan juseyo]

- **Hour** 시간 [sigan]

We wiill be back in 2 hours.

두 시간 후에 돌아오겠습니다.

[du sigan hu-e dora-ogesseumnida]

- **Housewife** 주부 [jubu]

I'm a housewife.

나는 주부입니다.

[naneun jubu-imnida]

- **Hungry** 배고픈 [baegopeun]

I'm hungry.

배가 고픕니다.

[baega gopeumnida]

- **Hurry** 서두르는, 빨리 [seodureneun, ppalri]

Hurry up, we are late.

서두르세요, 늦겠어요.

[seodureuseyo, neukkesseoyo]

- **Hurt** 다치다, 아프다 [dachida, apeuda]

You hurt me.

당신 때문에 아파요.

[dangsin ttaemune apayo]

- **Husband** 남편 [nampyeon]

My husband is caring.

내 남편은 자상합니다.

[nae nampyeoneun jasanghamnida]

- **Ice** 얼음 [eoreum]

  Give me some ice, please.

  얼음 주세요.

  [eoreum juseyo]

- **ID card** 신분증 [sinbunjeung]

  Can I see your ID card?

  신분증을 보여 주세요.

  [sinbunjeungeul boyeo juseyo]

- **Illegal** 불법적인 [bulbeopjeogin]

  Illegal parking lot

  불법 주차 구역

  [bulppeop jucha guyeok]

- **Imagination** 상상 [sangsang]

  Your imagination is outstanding.

  당신의 상상력이 풍부합니다.

  [dangsin-e sangsangnyeogi pungbuhamnida]

- **Immediately** 즉시 [jeuksi]

  Do it immediately!

  즉시 실천하세요.

  [jeukssi silcheonhaseyo]

- **Impolite** 무례한 [muryehan]

  That's impolite.

  그것은 무례한 행동입니다.

  [geugeoseun muryehan haengdong-imnida]

● **In** 안에 [an-e]

I am in the room.

나는 방안에 있습니다.
[naneun bangane isseumnida]

● **In advance** 미리 [miri]

Please, tell me in advance.

미리 말해 주세요.
[mirimiri malhae juseyo]

● **In the future** 앞으로 [apeuro]

What do you want to be in the future?

앞으로 무엇이 되고 싶어요?
[apeuro mu-eosi doegosipeoyo]

● **Income** 수입 [suip]

What is your annual income?

수입이 얼마 입니까?
[su-ibi eolma imnikka]

● **Industry** 산업 [saneop]

The Korean industry is growing.

한국의 산업은 발전하고 있습니다.
[hangug-e san-eobeun baljjeonhago isseumnida]

● **Inexpensive** 값싼 [gapssan]

This mall has inexpensive items.

이 쇼핑몰은 값이 싸군요.
[i syopingmoreun gapsi ssagunyo]

● **Infant** 영아 [yeonga]
This is infant formula.
영아용 분유입니다.
[yeong-ayong bunyu-imnida]

● **Information** 정보 [jeongbo]
Give me some information.
내게 정보를 주시겠어요?
[naege jeongboreul jusigesseoyo]

● **Information** 안내 [annae]
Go to the information desk.
안내 데스크로 가세요.
[annae deskeuro gaseyo]

● **Inside** 안에 [an-e]
The telephone is inside the entrance hall.
전화기는 출입구 안에 있습니다.
[jeonhwagineun churibkku ane isseumnida]

● **Insurance** 보험 [boheom]
Did you sign up for the insurance?
보험 가입하셨어요?
[boheom ga-ip hasyeosseoyo]

● **International** 국제적인 [gukjjejeogin]
Incheon Airport is the international airport.
인천 공항은 국제적인 공항입니다.
[incheon gonghangeun gukjjejeogin gonghang-imnida]

- **Internet** 인터넷 [inteonet]

  The internet is fast.

  인터넷 속도가 빠릅니다.

  [inteonet sokttoga ppareumnida]

- **Introduce** 소개하다 [sogaehada]

  Let me introduce myself.

  저를 소개하겠습니다.

  [jeoreul sogaehagesseumnida]

- **Invite** 초대하다 [chodaehada]

  I want to invite you.

  당신을 초대합니다.

  [dangsineul chodaehamnida]

- **Iron** 다리미 [darimi]

  I iron the skirt.

  다림질을 합니다.

  [darimjireul hamnida]

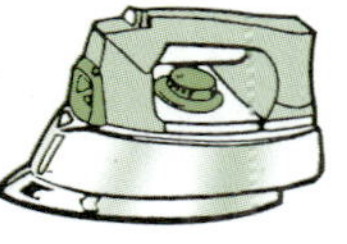

- **Island** 섬 [seom]

  I want to go to an island.

  섬에 가고 싶습니다.

  [seome gago sipsseumnida]

J

- **Jacket** 재킷 [jaekit]

  The jacket fits you.

  재킷이 잘 어울립니다.

  [jaekisi jal eo-ulrimnida]

● **Jam** 잼 [jaem]

We spread jam on the bread.

빵에 잼을 발라 먹습니다.
[ppang-e jaemeul balra meoksseumnida]

● **Japan** 일본 [ilbon]

I have been to Japan.

나는 일본에 가 본 적이 있습니다.
[naneun ilbone ga bon jeogi isseumnida]

● **Jealousy** 질투 [jiltu]

Godness, Hera is called 'the goddess of jealousy'.

헤라는 질투의 여신입니다.
[heraneun jiltu-e yeosinimnida]

● **Jeans** 청바지 [cheongbaji]

Jeans are comfortable.

청바지는 편합니다.
[cheongbajineun pyeonhamnida]

● **Jewelry** 보석 [boseok]

I have a lot of jewelry.

나는 보석이 많습니다.
[naneun boseogi manseumnida]

● **Job** 직업 [jigeob]

I am looking for a job.

직업을 구합니다.
[jigeobeul guhamnida]

● **Jogging** 조깅 [joging]

I am jogging now.

조깅하고 있어요.

[joginghago isseoyo]

● **Joke** 농담 [nongdam]

He loves to joke.

그는 농담을 잘 합니다.

[geuneun nongdameul jal hamnida]

● **Journey** 여행 [yeohaeng]

How's your journey?

여행은 어땠어요?

[yeohaengeun eottaesseoyo]

● **Judge** 판사 [pansa]

That judge makes justice.

그 판사는 공정합니다.

[geu pansaneun gongjeonghamnida]

● **Juice** 주스 [juseu]

What kinds of juice do you like?

어떤 주스를 좋아하세요?

[eotteon juseureul jo-ahaseyo]

K

● **Ketchup** 케첩 [kecheop]

Bring me the ketchup, please.

케첩 주시겠어요?

[kecheop jusigesseoyo]

- **Key** 열쇠 [yeolsoi]
  I found my key.
  열쇠를 찾았어요.
  [yeolsoereul chajasseoyo]

- **Kind** 친절한 [chinjeoran]
  He is kind.
  그는 친절합니다.
  [geuneun chinjeoramnida]

- **Kindergarten** 유치원 [yuchiwon]
  Kindergarten is fun.
  유치원은 재밌습니다.
  [yuchiwoneun jaemisseumnida]

- **Kiss** 키스 [kis]
  Can I kiss you?
  키스해도 될까요?
  [kiseuhaedo doelkkayo]

- **Kitchen** 주방 [jubang]
  That's in the kitchen.
  그것은 주방에 있어요.
  [geugeoseun jubang-e isseoyo]

- **Knife** 나이프, 칼 [naipeu, kal]
  Pass me the knife, please.
  나이프 주세요.
  [na-ipeu juseyo]

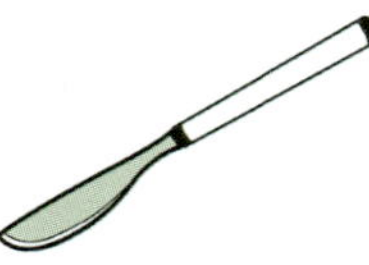

- **Know** 알다 [alda]

  Do you know?

  당신 알지요?

  [dangsin aljiyo]

- **Korea, the Republic of Korea** 한국, 대한민국 [hanguk, daehanminguk]

  I am from Korea.

  나는 한국에서 왔습니다.

  [naneun hangugeseo wasseumnica]

- **Korean** 한국 사람 [hanguk saram]

  I am Korean.

  나는 한국 사람입니다.

  [naneun hanguksaramimnida]

L

- **Lake** 호수 [hosu]

  The lake is calm.

  호수는 고요합니다.

  [hosuneun goyohamnida]

- **Large** 큰 [keun]

  Do you want a large cup?

  큰 컵으로 드릴까요?

  [keun keobeuro deurilkkayo]

- **Last** 마지막 [majimak]

  The last concert

  마지막 콘서트

  [majimak konsseotteu]

- **Late** 늦은 [neujeun]

  I'm late at school.

  학교에 늦었습니다.

  [hakyo-e neujeosseumnida]

- **Later** 나중에, 후에 [najunge, hue]

  I'll do it later.

  나중에 할께요.

  [najung-e halkkeyo]

- **Laundry** 세탁물 [setangmul]

  I have some laundry.

  세탁물이 있어요.

  [setangmuri isseoyo]

- **Law** 법 [beop]

  Don't break the law.

  법을 지켜야만 합니다.

  [beobeul jikyeoyaman hamnida]

- **Lawyer** 변호사 [byeonhosa]

  I want to be a lawyer.

  변호사가 되고 싶어요.

  [byeonhosaga doegosipeoyo]

- **Learn** 배우다 [baeuda]

  I learn from you.

  당신으로부터 배웁니다.

  [dangsineurobuteo bae-umnida]

- **Lecture** 강의 [gangeui]

The lecture is interesting.

강의 시간이 즐겁습니다.

[gang-ui sigani jeulgeopsseumnida]

- **Left** 왼쪽 [oenjjok]

It's on your left.

당신의 왼쪽에 있습니다.

[dangsin-e oenjjoge isseumnida]

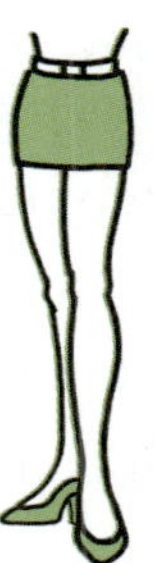

- **Leg** 다리 [dari]

She has beautiful legs.

그녀는 다리가 예쁩니다.

[geunyeoneun dariga yeppeumnida]

- **Leisure** 여가 [yeoga]

What do you do on your leisure time?

여가 시간에는 무얼 하십니까?

[yeoga siganeneun mu-eol hasimnikka]

- **Letter** 편지 [pyeonji]

I got a letter.

편지를 받았습니다.

[pyeonjireul badasseumnida]

- **Lettuce** 상추 [sangchu]

I want lettuce with my hambuger.

햄버거에 상추를 넣어주세요.

[haembeogeo-e sangchureul neo-eojuseyo]

- **Library** 도서관 [doseogwan]
  There are many books in the library.
  도서관에 책이 많습니다.
  [doseogwane chaegi mansseumnida]

- **License** 면허, 자격증 [myeonheo, jagyeokjeung]
  I have a driver's license.
  운전 면허증이 있습니다.
  [unjeon myeonheojjeung-i isseumnida]

- **Lie** 거짓말 [geojinmal]
  Don't lie.
  거짓말을 하지 마세요.
  [geojinmareul haji maseyo]

- **Lift** 들다 [deulda]
  The machine lifts up the rocks.
  기계로 바위를 들었습니다.
  [gigyero bawireul deureosseumnida]

- **Light** 불빛 [bulppit]
  The light is bright.
  불빛이 밝습니다.
  [bulppichi baksseumnida]

- **Lips** 입술 [ipsul]
  My lips are chapped.
  입술이 말랐어요.
  [ipsuri malrasseoyo]

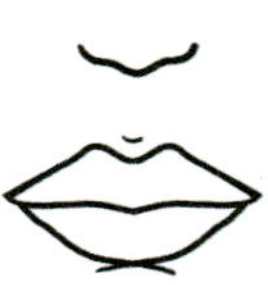

● **Literature** 문학 [munhak]

Korean literature is interesting.

한국 문학은 재미있습니다.

[hanguk munhageun jaemi-isseumnida]

● **Little** 조금 [jogeum]

Just a little short.

조금 모자랍니다.

[jogeum mojaramnida]

● **Live** 살다 [salda]

I live near the lake.

나는 호숫가에 삽니다.

[naneun hosukka-e samnida]

● **Lobby** 로비 [lobi]

The lobby is on the 1st floor.

로비는 일 층에 있습니다.

[lobineun il cheunge isseumnida]

● **Lobster** 바다 가재 [bada gajae]

Lobster is expensive.

바다 가재는 비쌉니다.

[bada gajaeneun bissamnida]

● **Lock** 자물쇠 [jamulsoe]

I put a key in a lock.

열쇠로 자물쇠를 열었습니다.

[yeolsoero jamulsoereul yeoreosseumnida]

- **Lose** 잃어버리다 [ireobeorida]

  I lost my wallet.

  지갑을 잃어버렸습니다.

  [jigabeul ireobeoryeosseumnida]

- **Love** 사랑 [sarang]

  Love is believing.

  사랑은 믿음입니다.

  [sarangeun mideumimnida]

- **Lucky** 운 좋은 [unjoeun]

  Today is such a lucky day.

  운 좋은 날입니다.

  [un jo-eun narimnida]

- **Luggage** 짐 [jim]

  Can you carry my luggage?

  짐을 날라 주시겠어요?

  [jimeul nalra jusigesseoyo]

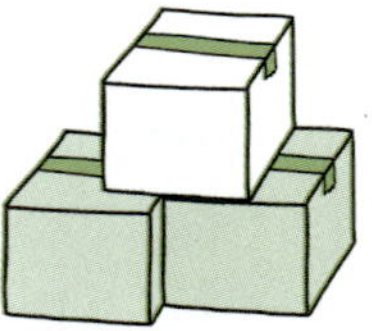

- **Lunch** 점심식사 [jeomsimsiksa]

  Did you have nice lunch?

  점심식사 맛있게 하셨어요?

  [jeomsimsikssa masikke hasyeosseoyo]

- **Luxurious** 고급스런 [gogeupseureon]

  Those are luxurious earings.

  고급스런 귀걸이입니다.

  [gogeupseureon gwigeori-imnida]

● **Machine** 기계 [gigye]

Do you have a vending machine?

자동판매기가 있습니까?

[jadongpanmaegiga isseumnikka]

● **Magazine** 잡지 [jabji]

This is a monthly magazine.

이 잡지는 한 달 마다 옵니다.

[i jabjineun han dal mada omnida]

● **Magic** 마술 [mabeob]

He does magic.

그는 마술을 합니다.

[geuneun masureul hamnida]

● **Maid** 파출부 [pachulbu]

I am looking for a maid.

나는 파출부를 찾고 있습니다.

[naneun pachulbureul chakko isseumnida]

● **Mail** 우편 [upyeon]

I've got mail.

우편을 받았습니다.

[upyeoneul badasseumnida]

● **Make** 만들다 [mandeulda]

Children love to make anything.

아이들은 만들기를 좋아합니다.

[aideureun mandeulgireul joahamnida]

- **Man** 남자 [namja]

  He is a nice man.

  그 남자는 좋은 분입니다.

  [geu namjaneun jo-eun bunimnida]

- **Manager** 매니저 [maenijeo]

  Where is a manager?

  매니저가 어디 있습니까?

  [maenijeoga eodi isseumnikka]

- **Map** 지도 [jido]

  This is the map of Korea.

  이것이 한국 지도 입니다.

  [igeosi hanguk jido-imnida]

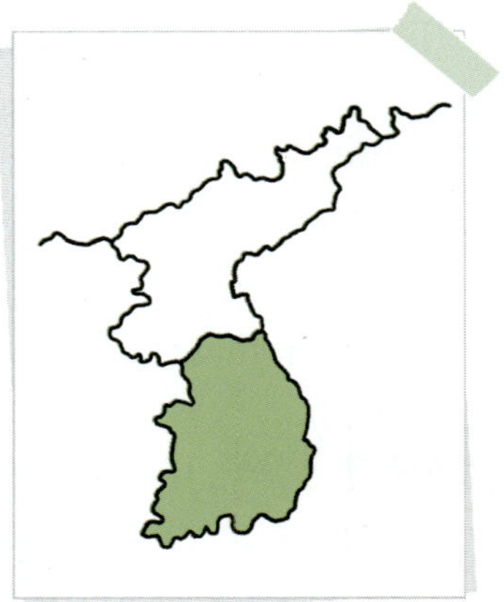

  - **City map** 시내 지도 [sinae jido]

    Seoul city map

    서울 시내 지도

    [Seoul sinae jido]

  - **Road map** 도로교통 지도 [dorogyotong jido]

    Metropolitan area road map

    중심가 도로 지도

    [jungsimga doro jido]

- **Market** 시장 [sijang]

  I'm looking for a traditional market.
  (= I'm looking for a market place)

  재래 시장이 어디입니까?

  [jaerae sijangi eodi-imnikka]

● **Marriage** 결혼 [gyeoron]

This is a marriage ring.

이것은 결혼반지 입니다.

[igeoseun gyeoron banji-imnida]

● **Martial arts** 무술 [musul]

Taekkwondo is Korean martial arts.

태권도는 한국의 무술입니다.

[taekwondoneun hanguge musurimnida]

● **Massage** 마사지, 안마 [matsaji, anma]

Thailand is famous for their massage.

태국은 마사지로 유명합니다.

[taegugeun massajiro yumyeonghamnida]

● **Math** 수학 [suhak]

Math is difficult.

수학은 어렵습니다.

[suhageun eoryeopsseumnida]

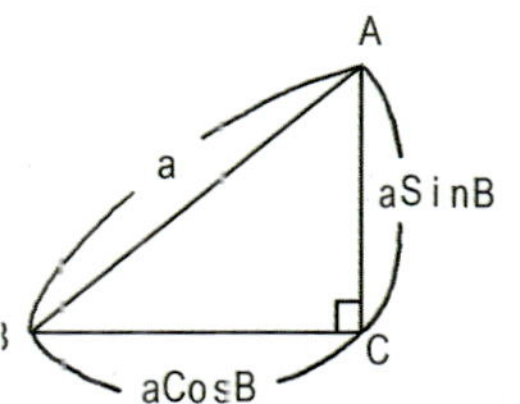

● **Mature** 성숙한 [seongsukan]

She is mature.

그녀는 성숙합니다.

[geunyeoneun seongsukamnida]

● **Meal** 식사 [sikssa]

Thank you for the meal.

식사 감사합니다.

[sikssa gamsahamnida]

● **Meat** 고기 [gogi]

Want some meat ?

고기 어때요?

[gogi eottaeyo]

● **Medical insurance** 의료보험 [uiryoboheom]

Can I see your medical insurance card?

의료보험 카드 보여 주세요.

[uiryoboheom kadeu boyeo juseyo]

● **Medicine** 약 [yag]

I took medicine.

약을 먹었습니다.

[yageul meogeosseumnida]

● **Meeting** 회의 [hoi-ui]

Where is the meeting held?

어디에서 회의가 있습니까?

[eodi-eseo hoe-uiga isseumnikka]

● **Menu** 메뉴 [menyu]

What's on the special menu today?

오늘의 특별 메뉴는 무엇입니까?

[oneure teukbyeol menyuneun mu-eosimnikka]

● **Message** 메시지 [metsiji]

Please, leave a message.

메시지를 남겨주세요.

[messijireul namgyeojuseyo]

- **Mexico**　멕시코　[megsiko]

  Taco is from Mexico.

  타코는 멕시코 음식입니다.

  [taconeun mekssiko eumsigimnida]

- **Midnight**　한밤중　[hanbamjung]

  I go to bed at midnight.

  나는 한밤중에 잠을 잡니다.

  [naneun hanbamjunge jameul jamnida]

- **Military**　군인　[gunin]

  It's a Korean youngmen's duty to do military service.

  한국 청년은 군인의 의무가 있습니다.

  [hanguk cheongnyeoneun gunine uimuga isseumnida]

- **Milk**　우유　[uyu]

  Milk does body good.

  우유는 몸에 좋아요.

  [uyuneun mome joayo]

- **Mineral water**　생수　[saengsu]

  One mineral water, please.

  생수 주세요.

  [saengsu juseyo]

- **Minimum**　최소한　[choisohan]

  Is this the minimum amount?

  최소한의 금액입니까?

  [choesohane geumaegimnikka]

- **Minute** 분 [bun]

  It takes a few minutes.

  몇 분 걸립니다.

  [myeot ppun georimnida]

- **Miracle** 기적 [gijeok]

  Do you believe in miracle?

  기적을 믿나요?

  [gijeogeul minnayo]

- **Mirror** 거울 [geoul]

  Mirror, mirror who is the most beautiful of all?

  거울아, 거울아, 누가 제일 예쁘니?

  [geo-ura, geo-ura, nuga jeil yeppeuni]

- **Miss., Mr., Mrs.** ~씨 [~ssi]

  The title that usually comes when we call the person

  사람을 부를 때 앞에 붙이는 말

  [sarameul bureul ttae ape buchineun mal]

- **Mistake** 실수 [silsu]

  It's my mistake.

  내 실수입니다.

  [nae silsu-imnida]

- **Mobile phone** 휴대폰 [hyudaepon]

  I got a new mobile phone.

  새 휴대폰을 샀습니다.

  [sae hyudaeponeul sasseumnida]

- **Modern** 현대의 [hyundaeeui]

  Modern technology is fast.

  현대의 과학 기술은 빠릅니다.

  [hyundae-ui gwahak gisureun ppareumnida]

- **Mom** 엄마 [eomma]

  I like my mom.

  나는 엄마가 좋아요.

  [naneun eommaga joayo]

- **Moment** 잠시 [jamsi]

  Wait a moment.

  잠시 기다리십시오.

  [jamsi gidarisipsiyo]

- **Money** 돈 [don]

  Can I borrow some money?

  돈 좀 빌려주세요.

  [don jom bilryeojuseyo]

- **Moon** 달 [dal]

  Look at the moon!

  달 좀 보세요.

  [dal jom boseyo]

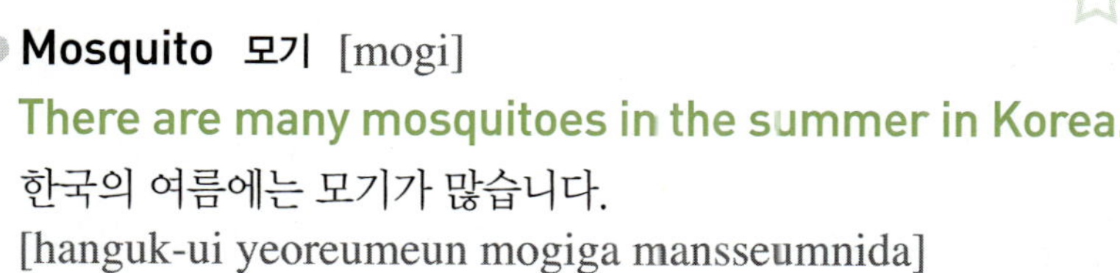

- **Mosquito** 모기 [mogi]

  There are many mosquitoes in the summer in Korea.

  한국의 여름에는 모기가 많습니다.

  [hanguk-ui yeoreumeun mogiga mansseumnida]

- **Motorcycle** 오토바이 [otobai]

Motorcycles have two wheels.

오토바이는 바퀴가 둘입니다.

[otobaineun bakwiga durimnida]

- **Mountain** 산 [san]

Mountains make up 70% of Korea.

한국은 칠십 퍼센트가 산입니다.

[hangugeun chilsip pesenteuga sanimnida]

- **Mouse** 쥐 [jwi]

The cat chases a mouse.

고양이는 쥐를 쫓아갑니다.

[goyangineun jwireul jjochagaminida]

- **Mouth** 입 [ib]

We eat with a mouth.

입으로 먹습니다.

[ibeuro meoksseumnida]

- **Movie** 영화 [yeonghwa]

Do you like movies?

영화 좋아 하세요?

[yeonghwa joahaseyo]

- **Much** 많은 [maneun]

Thank you very much.

많은 감사드립니다.

[maneun gamsadeurimnida]

- **Museum** 박물관 [bangmulgwan]

  There is a national museum in YongSan, Korea.

  용산에는 국립 박물관이 있습니다.

  [yongsaneneun gungnip bangmulgwani isseumnida]

- **Mushroom** 버섯 [beoseot]

  The mushroom is in the omelet. 

  오믈렛에 버섯이 들어 있습니다.

  [omulese beoseosi deureo issuemnida]

- **Music** 음악 [eumag]

  I like music.

  나는 음악을 좋아합니다.

  [naneun eumageul joahamnida]

- **Musician** 음악가 [eumakga]

  Mozart is the most famous musician ever.

  모차르트는 유명한 음악가입니다.

  [mochareuteuneun yumyeonghan eumakka-imnida]

- **Mustard** 겨자 [gyeoja]

  I need some mustard.

  나는 겨자가 필요합니다.

  [naneun gyeojaga piryohamnida]

● **My** 내, 나의 [nae, na-eui]

It's my car.
내 차입니다.
[nae cha-imnida]

This is my family.
나의 가족입니다.
[na-ui gajogimnida]

N

● **Nail clippers** 손톱깎이 [sontopkkakki]
Where are my nail clippers?
손톱깎이 어디 있어요?
[sontopkkakki eodi isseoyo]

● **Name** 이름 [ireum]
I want to have a Korean name.
한국 이름을 갖고 싶어요.
[hanguk ireumeul gakko sipeoyo]

● **Napkin** 냅킨 [naepkin]
The napkins are over there.
냅킨은 저기 있습니다.
[naepkineun jeogi isseumnida]

● **Near** 가까이 [gakkai]
I am near you.
당신 가까이에 있어요.
[dangsin gakka-ie isseoyo]

Neck 목 [mok]

A giraffe has a long neck.

기린은 목이 깁니다.

[girineun mogi gimnida]

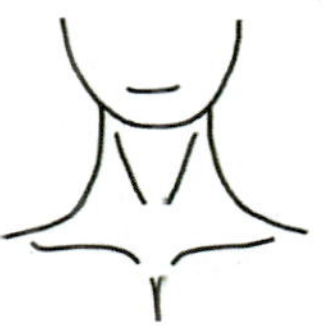

Need 필요 [piryo]

I don't need your help.

당신 도움 필요 없어요.

[dangsin doum piryo eopseoyo]

Neighbor 이웃 [iut]

My neighbor is nice.

우리 이웃은 친절합니다.

[uri iuseun chinjeoramnida]

New Year 새해 [saehae]

What's your New Year's resolution?

새해 소망이 무엇입니까?

[saehae somang-i mu-eosimnikka]

Next 다음 [da-eum]

What's next?

그 다음에는?

[geu da-eumeneun]

Night 밤 [bam]

It's chilly at night.

밤에는 쌀쌀합니다.

[bameneun ssalssaramnida]

- **Noodle** 국수 [guksu]

  I like noodle.

  국수를 좋아합니다.

  [guksureul jo-ahamnida]

- **Noon (12 o'clock)** 정오 [jeongo]

  Let' have lunch at noon.

  정오에 점심식사해요.

  [jeong-o-e jeomsimsikssahaeyo]

- **North** 북쪽, 북 [bukjjok, buk]

  There are East, West, North, and South.

  동, 서, 남, 북이 있습니다.

  [dong, seo, nam, bugi isseumnida]

- **Nose** 코 [ko]

  You smell with your nose.

  코로 냄새를 맡습니다.

  [koro naemsaereul matsseumnida]

- **Not** 아니다 [anida]

  Not at all.

  절대 아닙니다.

  [jeoldae animnida]

- **Now** 지금 [jigeum]

  I'm talking now.

  나는 지금 말하고 있습니다.

  [naneun jigeum marago isseumnida]

- **Number** 번호 [beonho]

What's your ID number?

ID 번호가 무엇입니까?

[ID beonhoga mu-eosimnikka]

- **Nurse** 간호사 [ganhosa]

Call the nurse, please.

간호사를 불러 주세요.

[ganhosareul bulreo juseyo]

- **Nuts** 견과류 [gyeongwaryu]

Nuts are good for your health.

견과류는 몸에 좋습니다.

[gyeongwaryuneun mome josseumnida]

O

- **Occupation** 일, 직업 [il, jigeop]

What's your father's occupation?

아버지의 직업은 무엇입니까?

[abeoji-e jigeobeun mu-eosimnikka]

- **Ocean** 대양 [daeyang]

The Atlantic Ocean is colder than the Pacific.

대서양은 태평양보다 추워요.

[daeseoyangeun taepyeongyangboda chuwoyo]

- **October** 시월 [siwol]

It's beautiful in October in Korea.

한국의 시월은 아름답습니다.

[hangug-e siworeun areumdapsseumnida]

- **Office** 사무실 [samusil]

  Where is the office key?

  사무실 열쇠가 어딨어요?

  [samusil yeolsoega eodisseoyo]

- **Old** 늙은 [neulgeun]

  That is an old dog.

  저 개는 늙은 개입니다.

  [jeo gaeneun neulgeun gae-imnida]

- **One** 하나, 한 [hana, han]

  Give me one.

  한 개 주세요.

  [han gae juseyo]

- **Onion** 양파 [yangpa]

  Peel off the onion skin.

  양파 껍질을 벗기세요.

  [yangpa kkeopjireul beokkiseyo]

- **Open** 열다 [yeolda]

  Open the door.

  문 여세요.

  [mun yeoseyo]

- **Orange** 오렌지 [orenji]

  'Gyul' stands for oranges in Korea.

  한국의 오렌지는 '귤' 입니다.

  [hangug-e orenjineun 'gyul' imnida]

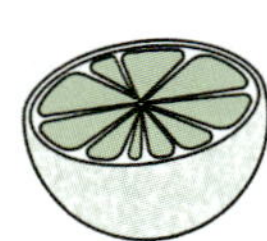

- **Our** 우리의 [urieui]

  Let's make our wishes.

  우리의 소원을 빌어요.

  [uri-e sowoneul bireoyo]

- **Outside** 밖 [bak]

  It's cold outside.

  밖은 춥습니다.

  [bakkeun chupsseumnida]

- **Owner** 주인 [juin]

  Who is the owner?

  주인이 누구세요?

  [ju-ini nuguseyo]

P

- **Package** 소포 [sopo]

  You got 2 packages.

  두 개의 소포가 있습니다.

  [dugae-e sopoga isseumnida]

- **Pain** 아픈 [apeun]

  I have a backpain.

  등이 아픕니다.

  [deung-i apeumnida]

- **Painter** 화가 [hwaga]

  The painter is famous.

  그 화가는 유명합니다.

  [geu hwaganeun yumyeonghamnida]

● **Paper** 종이, 서류 [jong-i, seoryu]

Do you have some paper clips?

종이 클립 있습니까?

[jong-i keulrip isseumnikka]

Why don't you do your paper work?

서류를 작성해 주세요.

[seoryureul jaksseonghae juseyo]

● **Parents** 부모님 [bumonim]

How are your parents?

부모님은 잘 지내세요?

[bumonimeun jal jinaeseyo]

● **Park** 공원, 주차 [gongwon, jucha]

The park is beautiful.

공원은 아름답습니다.

[gonwoneun areumdapsseumnida]

Where can I park?

어디에 주차할 수 있습니까?

[eodi-e juchahal su isseumnikka]

● **Passport** 여권 [yeogwon]

I found a passport.

여권을 찾았습니다.

[yeogwoneul chajasseumnida]

● **Peanuts** 땅콩 [ttangkong]

Do you want some peanuts?

땅콩 드시겠어요?

[ttangkong deusigesseoyo]

- **Pencil** 연필 [yeonpil]
  This pencil is easy to write with.
  이 연필은 잘 써집니다.
  [i yeonpireun jal sseojimnida]

- **People** 사람 [sarram]
  Korean people are kind.
  한국 사람은 친절합니다.
  [hanguk sarameun chinjeoramnida]

- **Period** 생리 [saengri]
  My period is regular.
  생리가 규칙적입니다.
  [saengniga gyuchikjeogimnida]

- **Personal** 개인의 [gaeineui]
  That's a personal problem.
  개인적인 문제입니다.
  [gae-injeogin munje-imnida]

- **Pillow** 베개 [begae]
  I like a flat pillow.
  낮은 베개가 좋습니다.
  [najeun begaega josseumnida]

- **Pineapple** 파인애플 [painaepleu]
  A pineapple is ripe.
  파인애플이 익었습니다.
  [painaepleuri igeosseumnida]

- **Pink** 분홍 [bunhong]
  You look good in pink.
  분홍이 잘 어울립니다.
  [bunhongi jal eo-ulrimnida]

- **Play** 놀다 [nolda]
  Children play a lot.
  아이들은 놀이를 많이 합니다.
  [aideureun norireul mani hamnida]

- **Poem** 시 [si]
  My poem will be published.
  내 시를 출판할 예정입니다.
  [nae sireul chulpanhal yejeong-imnida]

- **Police** 경찰 [gyeongchal]
  Korean police are strong.
  한국 경찰은 강합니다.
  [hanguk gyeongchareun ganghamnida]

- **Postcard** 엽서 [yeopseo]
  I sent the postcard.
  나는 엽서를 보냈습니다.
  [naneun yeopseoreul bonaesseumnida]

- **Potato** 감자 [gamja]
  French fries, please.
  튀긴 감자주세요.
  [twigin gamjajuseyo]

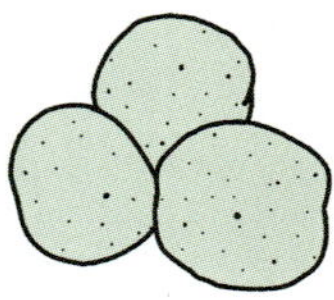

● **Present** 선물, 현재 [seonmul, hyeonjae]
I have a present for you.
선물을 준비했어요.
[seonmureul junbihaesseoyo]

I am a teacher at present.
나는 현재 선생님입니다.
[naneun hyeonjae seonsaengnimimnida]

● **Pretty** 예쁜 [yeppeun]
I am pretty.
나는 예쁩니다.
[naneun yeppeumnida]

● **Price** 가격 [gagyeog]
What's the price?
가격이 얼마입니까?
[gagyeogi eolma-imnikka]

● **Pride** 자부심 [jabusim]
I have pride.
나는 자부심이 있습니다.
[naneun jabusimi isseumnida]

● **Professor** 교수 [gyosu]
I want to be a professor.
교수가 되고 싶습니다.
[gyosuga doego sipsseumnida]

- **Profit** 이익 [i ik]

  I made some profit.

  이익을 냈습니다.

  [i igeul naesseumnida]

- **Promise** 약속 [yaksok]

  Can you promise me?

  나와 약속할 수 있어요?

  [nawa yaksoghal su isseoyo]

- **Province** 도 [do]

  There are 8 provinces in Korea.

  한국에는 8도가 있습니다.

  [hangugeneun pal doga isseumnida]

- **Pull** 당기다 [danggida]

  Pull it!

  당기세요!

  [danggiseyo]

- **Push** 밀다 [milda]

  Push it!

  미세요!

  [miseyo]

- **Put** 놓다 [notta]

  Put it down.

  내려 놓으세요.

  [naeryeo no-euseyo]

- **Quality** 질 [jil]
  The products are famous for their high quality.
  이 제품은 질이 좋습니다.
  [i jepumeun jiri josseumnida]

- **Quantity** 양 [yang]
  It is a small quantity.
  양이 적습니다.
  [yang-i jeoksseumnida]

- **Queen** 여왕 [yeowang]
  A queen has dignity.
  여왕은 위엄이 있습니다.
  [yeowangeun wi-eomi isseumnica]

- **Question** 질문 [jilmun]
  I have a question.
  질문 있어요.
  [jilmun isseoyo]

- **Quickly** 빨리 [ppalri]
  Come, quickly!
  빨리 오세요.
  [ppalri oseyo]

- **Quiet** 조용히 [joyonghi]
  Be quiet, please.
  조용히 해 주세요.
  [joyonghi hae juseyo]

- **Quit** 그만 두다 [geuman duda]

  I quit the job.

  일을 그만 두었습니다.

  [ireul geuman du-eosseumnida]

R

- **Rabbit** 토끼 [ttokki]

  A rabbit is fast.

  토끼는 빠릅니다.

  [tokkineun ppareumnida]

- **Rain** 비 [bi]

  Rain drops.

  비가 오기 시작합니다.

  [biga ogi sijakamnida]

- **Razor** 면도기 [myeondogi]

  I shave with a razor.

  면도기로 면도를 했습니다.

  [myoendogiro myeondoreul haesseumnida

- **Read** 읽다 [iltta]

  Can you read Korean (Hangeul)?

  한글을 읽을 줄 아십니까?

  [hangeureul ilgeul jul asimnikka]

- **Reason** 이유 [iyu]

  I want to know the reason.

  이유를 알고 싶어요.

  [iyureul algo sipeoyo]

● **Receipt** 영수증 [yeongsujeung]

Receipt, please.

영수증 주세요.

[yeongsujeung juseyo]

● **Red** 빨간 [ppalgan]

I bought a pair of red shoes.

빨간 구두를 샀습니다.

[ppalgan gudureul sasseumnida]

● **Refrigerator** 냉장고 [naengjanggo]

I want to buy a refrigerator.

냉장고를 사야겠어요.

[naengjanggoreul sayagesseoyo]

● **Refund** 환불 [hwanbul]

Can I get refund, please?

환불해 주시겠어요?

[hwanbulhae jusigesseoyo]

● **Rent** 빌리다 [bilrida]

I want to rent a house.

집을 빌리고 싶습니다.

[jibeul bilrigo sipsseumnida]

● **Rest** 휴식 [hyusik]

You need some rest.

당신은 휴식이 필요합니다.

[dangsineun hyusigi piryohamnida]

- **Restaurant** 음식점 [eumsikjjeom]

  This is a decent restaurant.

  참 맛있는 음식점입니다.

  [cham masinneun eumsikjeomimnida]

- **Restroom** 화장실 [hwajangsil]

  Where is the restroom?

  화장실이 어딨어요?

  [hwajangsiri eodisseoyo]

- **Resume** 이력서 [iryeoksseo]

  Send me a resume.

  이력서 보내 주세요.

  [iryeoksseo bonae juseyo]

- **Rice** 밥 [bap]

  Kroean people are fond of rice.

  한국 사람은 밥을 먹습니다.

  [hanguk sarameun babeul meoksseumnida]

- **Ring** 반지 [banji]

  This is a wedding ring.

  결혼 반지입니다.

  [gyeoron banji-imnida]

- **Ripe** 익은 [igeun]

  This persimmon isn't ripe.

  감이 익지 않았습니다.

  [gami ikjji anasseumnida]

● **Room** 방 [bang]

Can I have a room with a view?

전망 좋은 방 주세요.

[jeonmang jo-eun bang juseyo]

● **Rule** 규칙 [gyuchik]

Keep the rule.

규칙을 지킵시다.

[gyuchigeul jikipssida]

S

● **Safe** 안전한 [anjeonhan]

It's safe here.

여기는 안전해요.

[yeogineun anjeonhaeyo]

● **Sale** 판매 [panmae]

I am having a sale.

판매합니다.

[panmaehamnida]

● **Salt** 소금 [sogeum]

Pass me the salt, please.

소금 주시겠어요?

[sogeum jusigesseoyo]

● **Same** 같은 [gateun]

We have the same taste.

취향이 같습니다.

[chwihyang-i gasseumnida]

- **Say** 말하다 [mal-hada = marada]

  Say, you love me.

  사랑한다고 말해 주세요.

  [saranghandago marae juseyo]

- **School** 학교 [hakkyo]

  It's time to go to school.

  학교 갈 시간입니다.

  [hakkyo gal siganimnida]

- **Sea** 바다 [bada]

  The East sea belongs to Korea.

  동해는 한국의 바다입니다.

  [donghaeneun hangug-e bada-imnida]

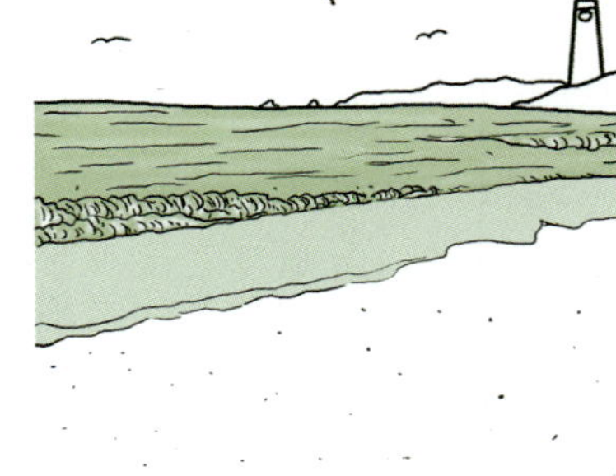

- **Seafood** 해산물 [haesanmul]

  Do you like seafood?

  해산물 요리 좋아하세요?

  [haesanmul yori joahaseyo]

- **Season** 계절 [gyejeol]

  What season do you like the most?

  어떤 계절을 좋아 하세요?

  [eotteon gyejeoreul joahaseyo]

- **Seat belt** 안전 벨트 [anjeon belteu]

  Fasten your seat belt.

  안전 벨트를 하세요.

  [anjeon belteureul haseyo]

- **Seaweed** 미역 [miyeok]

  We have seaweed soup on one's birthday in Korea.

  한국에서는 생일날 미역국을 먹습니다.

  [hangugeseoneun saeng-ilral miyeokkueul meoksseumnida]

- **See** 보다 [boda]

  I can see you.

  당신 모습이 보여요.

  [dangsin moseubi boyeoyo]

- **Self service** 셀프 서비스 [sselpeu sseobiseu]

  It requires self service here.

  여기는 셀프 서비스입니다.

  [yeogineun sselpeu sseobiseu-imnida]

- **Sell** 팔다 [palda]

  Do you sell this item?

  이 물건 파는 겁니까?

  [i mulgeon paneun geomnikka]

- **Send** 보내다 [bonaeda]

  I will send you a postcard.

  엽서를 보낼 겁니다.

  [yeopsseoreul bonael geomnida]

- **Service** 봉사 [bongsa]

  One dollar for the service charge.

  봉사료는 1 달러입니다.

  [bongsaryoneun il dalleo-imnida]

- **Sex** 성, 섹스 [seong, sseksseu]

  They had sex.

  그들은 섹스를 했습니다.

  [geudeureun sseksseureul haesseumnida]

- **She** 그녀 [geunyeo]

  She is attractive.

  그녀는 매력적입니다.

  [geunyeoneun maeryeokjjeogimnida]

- **Shoes** 신발 [sinbal]

  There is a shoe store.

  저기가 신발 가게입니다.

  [jeogiga sinbal gage-imnida]

- **Shop** 가게 [gage]

  I need to stop by the shop.

  가게에 들러야 합니다.

  [gage-e deulreoya hamnida]

- **Shopping** 쇼핑 [syoping]

  I love shopping.

  나는 쇼핑을 좋아합니다.

  [naneun syopingeul joahamnida]

- **Short** 짧은 [jjalbeun]

  This is a short story.

  이것은 짧은 이야기입니다.

  [igeoseun jjalbeun iyagi-imnida]

- **Show** 보이다 [boida]

  Show me your intention. (= true feelings)

  당신의 진심을 보여주세요.

  [dangsin-e jinsimeul boyeojuseyo]

- **Shy** 수줍은 [sujubeun]

  I'm shy.

  나는 수줍어 합니다.

  [naneun sujubeo hamnida]

- **Sick** 아픈 [apeun]

  Are you sick?

  당신 아픕니까?

  [dangsin apeumnikka]

- **Side** 옆에 [yeope]

  It's on your right side.

  그것은 당신 오른쪽 옆에 있어요.

  [geugeseun dangsin oreunjjok yeope isseoyo]

- **Signature** 서명 [seomyeong]

  Be sure to get the signature.

  서명을 받으세요.

  [seomyeong-eul badeuseyo]

- **Sightseeing** 관광 [gwan-gwang]

  Do you want to go sightseeing?

  관광을 하고 싶습니까?

  [gwan-gwang-eul hago sipseumnikka]

- **Silk** 비단, 실크 [bidan, ssilkeu]
  Do you know "The Silk Road"?
  실크 로드를 아세요?
  [ssilkeu rodeureul aseyo]

- **Silver** 은 [eun]
  Korea is famous for silver craftwork.
  한국의 은공예는 유명합니다.
  [hangug-e eungongyeneun yumyeonghamnida]

- **Simple** 간단한 [gandanhan]
  It's simple.
  간단하군요.
  [gandanhagunyo]

- **Sing** 노래하다 [noraehada]
  The birds sing.
  새들은 노래합니다.
  [saedeuren noraehamnida]

- **Single** 독신 [dokssin]
  I am a single.
  나는 독신입니다.
  [naneun dokssinimnida]

- **Sister** 여자 형제 (자매) [yeoja hyeongje (jamae)]
  My sister is a college student.
  내 여자 형제는 대학생입니다.
  [nae yeoja hyeongjeneun daehaksaeng-imnida]

● **Sit** 앉다 [antta]

Where do you want to sit?

어디에 앉을까요?

[eodi-e anjeulkkayo]

● **Size** 사이즈, 크기 [ssaijeu, keugi]

Do you have another size (keugi)?

다른 사이즈(크기) 있습니까?

[dareun ssaijeu (keugi) isseumnikka]

● **Skirt** 치마, 스커트 [chima, seukeoteu]

I love skirts.

나는 치마를 좋아합니다.

[naneun chimareul joahamnida]

● **Sky** 하늘 [haneul]

The sky is blue.

하늘은 푸릅니다.

[haneureun pureumnida]

● **Sleep** 잠, 자다 [jam, jada]

Did you sleep tight?

안녕히 주무셨어요?

[annyeonghi jumusyeosseoyo]

● **Slow** 천천히, 슬로우 [cheoncheonhi , seulou]

'Slow food' is getting popular in Korea.

한국에서는 'slow food' 가 인기입니다.

[hangugeseoneun 'slow food' ga inkki-imnida]

● **Small** 작은 [jageun]

Give me a small plate.

작은 접시 주세요.

[jageun jeopsi juseyo]

● **Smile** 미소 [miso]

She has a beautiful smile.

그녀의 미소가 아름답습니다.

[geunyeo-ui misoga areumdapsseumnida]

● **Smoking area** 흡연 구역 [heubyeon guyeok]

Where is the smoking area?

흡연 구역이 어디입니까?

[heubyeon guyeogi eodi-imnikka]

● **Snow** 눈 [nun]

There is a lot of snow in winter.

겨울에는 눈이 많이 내립니다.

[gyeoureneun nuni mani naerimnida]

● **Soap** 비누 [binu]

Soap is slippery.

비누는 미끄럽습니다.

[binuneun mikkeureopsseumnida]

● **Socks** 양말 [yangmal]

Take off your socks.

양말을 벗어요.

[yangmareul beoseoyo]

- **Sometimes** 때때로 [ttaettaero]

  I sometimes feel blue.

  나는 때때로 우울합니다.

  [naneun ttaettaero u-ul-hamnida]

- **Song** 노래 [norae]

  Song by children are nice.

  아이들의 노래는 좋습니다.

  [aideure noraeneun josseumnida]

- **Soon** 즉시, (곧) [jeuksi (got)]

  He's coming soon.

  그는 즉시(곧) 옵니다.

  [geuneun jeukssi(got) omnida]

- **Soup** 수프 [supeu]

  I like onion soup.

  나는 양파 수프를 좋아합니다.

  [naneun yangpa supeureul joahamnida]

- **South** 남쪽 [namjjog]

  Jeju island is in the South.

  제주도는 남쪽에 있습니다.

  [jejudoneun namjjoge isseumnida]

- **Speak** 말하다 [mal-hada]

  You speak Korean fluently.

  당신의 한국어는 훌륭하군요.

  [dangsine hangugeoneun hulryunghagunyo]

- **Speed** 속도 [sokdo]

  Speed up!

  속도를 내세요!

  [sokdoreul naeseyo]

- **Spend** ~을 소비하다 (보내다) [~eul sobihada = bonaeda]

  I spend my vacations in Canada.

  나는 캐나다에서 휴가를 보냅니다.

  [naneun kaenada-eseo hyugareul bonaemnida]

- **Spoon** 숟가락 [sutkkarak]

  We use a spoon for rice.

  우리는 숟가락으로 밥을 먹습니다.

  [urineun sutkkarageuro babeul meoksseumnida]

- **Station** 역 [yeok]

  We're getting off at the next station.

  다음 역에서 내립니다.

  [da-eum yeogeseo naerimnida]

- **Steak** 스테이크 [seuteikeu]

  I decided to have steak.

  스테이크로 결정했습니다.

  [seuteikeuro gyeoljjeonghaesseumnida]

- **Stomach** 배 [bae]

  I have a stomach ache.

  배가 아픕니다.

  [baega apeumnida]

- **Stone** 돌 [dol]

  I collect stones.

  나는 돌을 수집합니다.

  [naneun doreul sujipamnida]

- **Stop** 정지 [jeongji]

  There is a stop sign.

  정지신호입니다.

  [jeongji sinho-imnida]

- **Straight** 곧장 [gotjjang]

  Don't go straight.

  곧장 가지 마세요.

  [gotjjang gaji maseyo]

- **Stranger** 낯선 사람 [natsseon saram]

  I am nervous with a stranger.

  낯선 사람 앞에선 긴장합니다.

  [natsseon saram apeseon ginjanghamnida]

- **Strawberries** 딸기 [ttalgi]

  Please, grind the strawberries.

  딸기를 갈아 주세요.

  [ttalgireul gara juseyo]

- **Street** 거리 [geori]

  There are many trees on the street.

  거리에 나무가 많습니다.

  [geori-e namuga manseumnida]

- **Strong** 강한 [ganghan]

  Koreans are strong. (= Koreans have strong will)

  한국 사람은 의지가 강합니다.
  [hanguk sarameun uijiga ganghamnida]

- **Student** 학생 [hakssaeng]

  Korean students study hard.

  한국 학생은 열심히 공부합니다.
  [hanguk hakssaengeun yeolssimi gongbuhamnida]

- **Subway** 전철, 지하철 [jeoncheol, jihachol]

  Here is a subway map.

  지하철 (전철) 지도입니다.
  [jihacheol(jeoncheol) jido-imnida]

- **Success** 성공 [seonggong]

  He made a success.

  그는 성공했습니다.
  [geuneun seonggonghaesseumnida]

- **Summer** 여름 [yeoreum]

  My summer vacation is short.

  여름 휴가가 짧습니다.
  [yereum hyugaga jjalseumnida]

- **Sun** 해, 태양 [hae (taeyang)]

  The sun is hot.

  태양이 (해가) 뜨겁습니다.
  [taeyang-i (haega) tteugeopsseumnida]

● **Sweat** 땀 [ttam]

I sweat a lot in summer.

여름에는 땀을 많이 흘립니다.

[yeoreumeneun ttameul mani heulrimnida]

● **Sweet** 단 [dan]

Mangos are sweet fruit.

망고는 단 과일 입니다.

[mangoneun dan gwail-imnida]

● **Swim** 수영하다 [suyeonghada]

I often go swimming. (= I often swim)

나는 자주 수영하러 갑니다.

[naneun jaju suyeonghareo gamnida]

● **Swimsuit** 수영복 [suyeongbok]

She wore swimsuit.

그녀는 수영복을 입었습니다.

[geunyeoneun suyeongbogeul ibeosseumnida]

T

● **Table** 테이블 (탁자) [te-ibeul (takjja)]

Clean up the table.

테이블(탁자)을 깨끗하게 하세요.

[te-ibeul(takjja)reul kkaekkeutage haseyo]

● **Take** 가져가다 [gajyeogada]

I'll take it.

가져 갈게요.

[gajyeo galkkeyo]

● **Tall** 큰 [keun]

You are tall.

당신은 크군요.

[dangsineun keugunyo]

● **Taxi** 택시 [taekssi]

There are many taxies in Korea.

한국에는 택시가 많습니다.

[hangugeneun taekssiga manseumnida]

● **Tea** 차 [cha]

Korean green tea is good for your health.

한국의 녹차는 몸에 좋습니다.

[hanguge nokchaneun mome josseumnida]

● **Teacher** 선생님 [seonsaengnim]

I respect teachers. (= I have respect for teachers.)

나는 선생님을 존경합니다.

[naneun seonsaengnimeul jon-gyeonghamnida]

● **Teeth** 치아 [chia]

My teeth are shiny.

내 치아는 반짝입니다.

[nae chianeun banjjagimnida]

● **Telephone** 전화 [jeonhwa]

Where is the public telephone?

공중 전화는 어디 있습니까?

[gongjung jeonhwaneun eodi isseumnikka]

- **Television** 텔레비전 [telebijeon]

The quality of Korean televisions is really high.

한국산 TV는 품질이 매우 좋습니다.

[hangukssan TVneun pumjiri mae-u josseumnida]

- **Temple** 절 [jeol]

Temples are usually located in mountains.

절은 주로 산에 많이 있습니다.

[jeoreun juro sane mani isseumnida]

- **Test** 시험 [siheom]

I hate tests.

나는 시험이 싫어요.

[naneun siheomi sireoyo]

- **Thank you** 고맙습니다 [gomapseumnida]

‘Thank you’ is a magic word.

‘Thank you’는 ‘마법 단어’ 입니다.

[‘ttaengkyu’neun ‘mabeob daneo’imnida]

- **That** 그, 그것 [geu, geugeot]

That's mine.

그것은 내 것입니다.

[geugeoseun nae geosimnida]

- **They** 그들 [geudeul]

They are my family.

그들은 내 가족입니다.

[geudeureun nae gajogimnida]

- **Thing** 것 [geot]

  That is such a good thing.

  좋은 것이네요.

  [jo-eun geosineyo]

- **Think** 생각하다 [saenggakhada]

  I think so.

  나도 그렇게 생각합니다.

  [nado geureoke saenggakamnida]

- **Thirsty** 목마른 [mongmareun]

  Give me some water, I'm thirsty.

  목이 말라요. 물 주세요.

  [mogi malrayo, mul juseyo]

- **Throat** 목구멍 [mogumeong]

  I have a sore throat.

  목구멍이 아파요.

  [mokkumeongi apayo]

- **Thursday** 목요일 [mogyoil]

  Today is Thursday.

  오늘은 목요일입니다.

  [oneureun mogyo-irimnida]

- **Ticket** 표 [pyo]

  Did you get a ticket?

  표 구하셨어요?

  [pyo guhasyeosseoyo]

● **Tired** 피곤한 [pigonhan]

I'm tired.

나는 피곤합니다.
[naneun pigonhamnida]

● **Today** 오늘 [oneul]

How's your today? (= How is today going so far?)

오늘 잘 지내셨어요?
[oneul jal jinaesyeosseoyo]

● **Toe** 발가락 [balkkarak]

My toes are cute.

발가락이 귀엽습니다.
[balkkaragi gwiyeopsseumnida]

● **Together** 함께 [hamkke]

Let's go together.

함께 가요.
[hamkke gayo]

● **Toilet** 변기 [byeongi]

The toilet is clean.

변기가 깨끗합니다.
[byeongiga kkaekkeutamnida]

● **Tomorrow** 내일 [naeil]

What are you doing tomorrow?

내일은 뭐 하세요?
[nae-ileun mwo haseyo]

● **Tonight** 오늘밤 [oneulpam]

I am hanging out with a friend tonight.

오늘 밤 친구와 만납니다.
[oneul pam chinguwa mannamnida]

● **Tour** 관광 [gwan-gwang]

There is a city tour bus.

시내 관광버스가 있습니다.
[sinae gwan-gwang beoseuga isseumnida]

● **Tourist** 관광객 [gwan-gwangaek]

Many tourists visit Jeju.

많은 관광객들이 제주를 방문합니다.
[maneun gwan-gwanggaekdeuri Jejureul bangmunhamnida]

● **Towel** 수건 [sugeon]

A white towel, please.

하얀색 수건 주세요.
[hayansaek sugeon juseyo]

● **Train** 기차, 열차 [gicha, yeolcha]

A train is long.

기차는 깁니다.
[gichaneun gimnida]

● **Transfer** 갈아타다 [garatada]

You have to transfer.

갈아타야만 합니다.
[garatayaman hamnida]

- **Travel** 여행하다 [yeohaenghada]

  I want to travel all around the world.

  세계 여행을 하고 싶어요.

  [segye yeohaengeul hago sipeoyo]

- **Tree** 나무 [namu]

  There are many trees in the garden.

  정원에 많은 나무가 있습니다.

  [jeongwone maneun namuga isseumnnida]

- **Trip** 여행 [yeohaeng]

  Have a good trip.

  좋은 여행 되세요.

  [jo-eun yeohaeng doeseyo]

- **Tuesday** 화요일 [hwayoil]

  Today is Tuesday.

  오늘은 화요일입니다.

  [oneureun hwayo-irimnida]

- **Tuna** 참치 [chamchi]

  Tuna is nutritious.

  참치는 영양이 풍부합니다.

  [chamchineun yeong-yangi pungbuhamnida]

- **Turkey** 칠면조 [chilmyeonjo]

  I'm cooking a turkey.

  칠면조 요리를 합니다.

  [chilmyeonjo yorireul hamnida]

- **Typoon** 태풍 [taepung]

  Typhoon is dangerous.

  태풍은 위험합니다.

  [taepung-eun wiheomhamnida]

U

- **Umbrella** 우산 [usan]

  Take the umbrella with you.

  우산 챙겨 가세요.

  [usan chaengyeo gaseyo]

- **Under** ~아래에 [~arae]

  Under the tree

  나무 아래에

  [namu arae-e]

- **Understand** 이해하다 [ihaehada]

  I understand what you're saying.

  무슨 말인지 알겠어요.

  [museun marinji algesseoyo]

- **Underwear** 속옷 [sogot]

  Change your underwear.

  속옷을 갈아 입으세요.

  [sogoseul gara ibeuseyo]

- **Unfair** 불공평한 [bulgongjeonghan]

  That is unfair.

  불공평 합니다.

  [bulgongpyeong hamnida]

● **Unhappy** 불행한 [buraenghan]

This is an unhappy news.

불행한 뉴스입니다.

[buraenghan nyusseu-imnida]

● **Uniform** 제복 [jebok]

The soldiers wear a uniform.

군인은 제복을 입습니다.

[gunineun jebogeul ipsseumnida]

● **Unique** 독특한 [dogteukan]

The design is unique.

디자인이 독특합니다.

[dija-ini dokteukamnida]

● **University** 대학교 [daehakkyo]

He goes to university.

그는 대학생입니다.

[geuneun daehakssaengimnida]

● **Untrue** 거짓인 [geojisin]

The story is untrue.

그 이야기는 거짓입니다.

[geu iyagineun geojisimnida]

● **Up** 위 [wi]

Up and down

위로 아래로

[wiro arae-ro]

- **Use** 사용하다 [sayonghada]

  Use the pencil.

  연필을 사용하세요.

  [yeonpireul sayonghaseyo]

V

- **Vacancy** 빈 [bin]

  No vacancy

  빈 방 없음.

  [binbang eopsseum]

- **Vacation** 휴가 [hyuga]

  What do you do during your vacation?

  이번 휴가에는 무엇을 하세요?

  [ibeon hyuga-eneun mu-eoseul haseyo]

- **Valley** 골짜기 [goljjagi]

  The stream runs in the valley.

  골짜기에는 물이 흐릅니다.

  [goljjagieneun muri heureumnida]

- **Valuable** 가치 있는 [gachi-inneun]

  Our heritage is valuable.

  문화재는 가치 있습니다.

  [muhwajaeneun gachi isseumnida]

- **Vegetable** 채소 [chaeso]

  Vegetable is good for your health.

  채소는 건강에 좋습니다.

  [chaesoneun geon-gang-e josseumnida]

Vending machine 자동 판매기 [jadong panmaegi]

Where is the vending machine?

자동 판매기는 어디 있습니까?

[jadongpanmaegineun eodi isseumnikka]

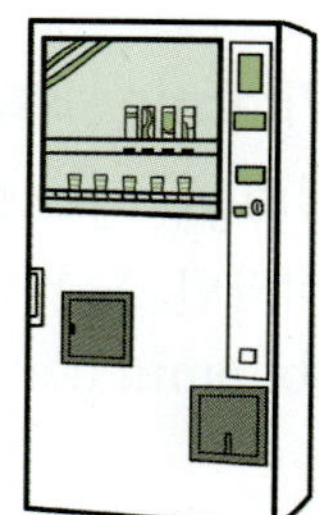

Very 매우 [maeu]

Thank you very much.

매우 고맙습니다.

[mae-u gomapsseumnida]

Vest 조끼 [jokki]

We wear a vest.

조끼를 입습니다.

[jokkireul ipsseumnida]

View 경치 [gyeongchi]

A room with a view

경치 좋은 방

[gyeongchi jo-eun bang]

Vinegar 식초 [sikcho]

Vinegar is sour.

식초는 십니다.

[sikchoneun simnida]

Visa 비자 [bija]

Do you have a visa?

비자 있습니까?

[bija isseumnikka]

● **Vitamin** 비타민 [bitamin]

Did you take vitamins?

비타민 드셨어요?

[bitamin deusyeosseoyo]

● **Vocabulary** 어휘 [eohwi]

Your vocabulary is rich.

어휘가 풍부하군요.

[eohwiga pungbuhagunyo]

W

● **Wait** 기다리다 [gidarida]

Wait up!

기다려요!

[gldaryeoyo]

● **Wake** 깨다 [kkaeda]

I wake him up!

그를 깨웠습니다.

[geureul kkaewosseumnida]

● **Walk** 걷다 [geotta]

I walk to school.

학교에 걸어서 갑니다.

[hakkyo-e georeoseo gamnida]

● **Wallet** 지갑 [jigap]

I got a wallet as a gift.

지갑을 선물 받았습니다.

[jigabeul seonmul badasseumnida]

● **Want**　~을 원하다, ~을 필요로 하다　[~eul wonhada, ~eul piryorohada]

I want a boyfriend.

남자친구를 원합니다.

[namjachigureul wonhamnida]

● **Warm**　따뜻한　[ttatteutan]

It's warm today.

오늘 따뜻합니다.

[oneul ttatteutamnida]

● **Wash**　~을 씻다　[~eul ssitta]

Wash the dishes.

접시를 씻으세요.

[jeopssireul ssiseuseyo]

● **Washroom**　화장실　[hwajangsil]

Here is the washroom.

여기가 화장실입니다.

[yeogiga hwajangsirimnida]

● **Watch**　시계　[sigye]

I need a watch.

시계가 필요해요.

[sigyega piryohaeyo]

● **Water**　물　[mul]

Water is important.

물은 중요합니다.

[mureun jungyohamnida]

- **Watermelon** 수박 [subak]

Do you have a watermelon?

수박 있어요?

[subak isseoyo]

- **Way** 길 [gil]

Is this right way?

이 길 맞아요?

[i gil majayo]

- **Weather** 날씨 [nalssi]

How's the weather?

날씨가 어때요?

[nalssiga eottaeyo]

- **Wedding** 결혼 [gyeoron]

Tomorrow is my wedding day.

내일은 결혼하는 날입니다.

[nae-ireun gyeoronhaneun narimnida]

- **Week** 주 [ju]

I go to the mountains everyweek.

매 주일마다 산에 갑니다.

[mae ju-ilmada sane gamnida]

- **Weight** 무게 [muge]

What's your weight?

몸무게가 얼마나 됩니까?

[mommugega eolmana doemnikka]

- **Welcome** 환영합니다. [hwanyeonghamnida]
  Welcome to Korea!
  한국에 오신 것을 환영합니다.
  [hanguge osingeoseul hwanyeonghamnida]

- **West** 서쪽 [seojjok]
  The sun sets in the West.
  해는 서쪽으로 집니다.
  [haeneun seojjogeuro jimnida]

- **White** 하얀색 [hayansaek]
  I am wearing white pants.
  하얀색 바지를 입었습니다.
  [hayansaek bajireul ibeosseumnida]

- **Why** 왜 [wae]
  Why not?
  왜 안 되지요?
  [wae an doejiyo]

- **Wife** 아내 [anae]
  Is she your wife?
  당신의 아내입니까?
  [dangsine anae-imnikka]

- **Wind** 바람 [baram]
  Wind blows.
  바람이 붑니다.
  [barami bumnida]

- **Window** 창문 [changmun]
  Open the window, please.
  창문을 열어 주시겠어요?
  [changmuneul yeoreo jusigesseoyo]

- **Wine** 포도주, (와인) [podoju, (wain)]
  A bottle of red wine, please.
  적포도주(레드 와인) 한 병 주세요.
  [jeokpodoju(red wain) han byeong juseyo]

- **Winter** 겨울 [gsyeoul]
  Let's go skiing in winter.
  겨울에 스키 타러 갈까요?
  [gyeoure seuki tareo galkkayo]

- **Wireless** 무선 [museon]
  It's a wireless telephone.
  무선 전화기입니다.
  [museon jeonhwagi-imnida]

- **With** ～와 함께 [~wa hamkke]
  I drink milk with bread.
  빵과 함께 우유를 마십니다.
  [ppanggwa hamkke uyureul masimnida]

- **Woman** 여자 [yeoja]
  That woman is warm hearted.
  그 여자는 마음이 따뜻합니다.
  [geu yeojaneun ma-eumi ttatteutamnida]

● **Wood** 나무 [namu]

The house is made of wood.

그 집은 나무로 지었습니다.

[geu jibeun namuro ji-eosseumnida]

● **Work** 일하다 [ilhada]

Where do you work?

어디에서 일하십니까?

[eodi-eseo ilhasimnikka]

● **Workplace** 일터 [ilteo]

Where's your workplace?

일터가 어디십니까?

[ilteoga eodisimnikka]

● **World** 세계 [segye]

Traveling in the world

세계 일주

[segye iljju]

● **Worry** 걱정 [geogjjeong]

No worries.

걱정하지 마세요.

[geokjjeonghaji maseyo]

● **Write** 쓰다 [sseuda]

I write a novel .

나는 소설을 씁니다.

[naneun soseoreul sseumnida]

- **Wrong** 틀린 [tteulrin]

  That is wrong.

  틀렸습니다.

  [tteulryeosseumnida]

X

- **X-ray** 엑스레이 [eks rei]

  I have a chest X-Ray.

  가슴 엑스레이를 찍었습니다.

  [gaseum ekseure-ireul jjigeosseumnida]

- **Xylophone** 실로폰 [sillopon]

  That xylophone is cute.

  실로폰이 귀엽습니다.

  [silloponi gwiyeopsseumnida]

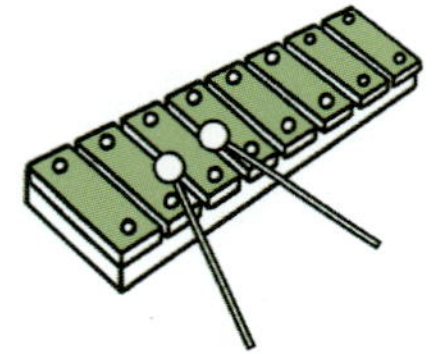

Y

- **Yard** 마당 [madang]

  I have a small yard.

  작은 마당이 있습니다.

  [jageun madang-i isseumnida]

- **Year** 해, 연도 [hae, yeondo]

  What year is it?

  올 해 연도가 어떻게 되지요?

  [ol hae yeondoga eotteoke doejiyo]

- **Yellow** 노랑 [norang]

  I like yellow.

  나는 노랑을 좋아합니다.

  [naneun norang-eul joahamnida]

- **Yes** 예 [ye]

  Yes, or no?

  예 또는 아니오?

  [ye ttoneun anio]

- **Yesterday** 어제 [eoje]

  I finished the homework yesterday.

  어제 숙제를 끝냈습니다.

  [eoje sukjjereul kkeunnaesseumnida]

- **Yet** 아직 [ajik]

  I haven't started yet.

  아직 시작을 못했습니다.

  [ajik sijageul mottaesseumnida]

- **Young** 젊은 [jeolmeun]

  I'm young.

  나는 젊습니다.

  [naneun jeomseumnida]

Z

- **Zero (0)** 영 [yeong (0)]

  It's below zero degree today.

  오늘은 영(0) 도 이하입니다.

  [oneureun yeong (0) do iha-imnida]

Zipper 지퍼 [jipeo]

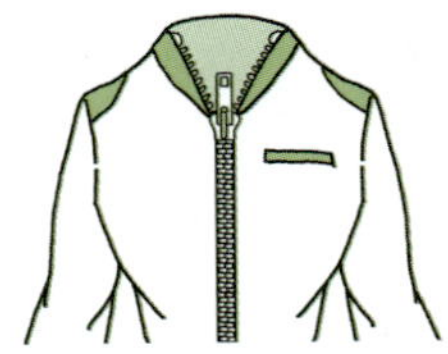

My zipper is broken.
지퍼가 고장입니다.
[jipeoga gojang-imnida]

Zone 구역 [guyeok]

There is DMZ (demilitarized zone) in Korea.
한국에는 DMZ가 있습니다.
[hangugeneun DMZga isseumnida]

Zoo 동물원 [dongmurwon]

Shall we go to zoo?
동물원에 갈까요?
[dongmurwone galkkayo]

한국어 어휘

hangugeo eohwi ㄱ - ㅎ

ㄱ

- 가게 [ga-ge] Shop / Store
- 가격 [ga-gyeok] Price
- 가까운 [ga-kka-un] Near
- 가능한 [ga-neung-han] Possible
- 가다 [ga-da] Go / Advance
- 가득채우다 [ga-deuk-chae-u-da] Fill up
- 가루 [ga-ru] Powder
- 가방 [ga-bang] Bag
- 가볍다 [ga-byeop-da] Light
- 가수 [ga-su] Singer
- 가슴 [ga-seum] Breast / Chest
- 가요 [ga-yo] Song
- 가을 [ga-eul] Autumn
- 가이드 [ga-i-deu] Guide
- 가족 [ga-jok] Family
- 가치 [ga-chi] Value
- 간판 [gan-pan] Signboard
- 갈등 [gal-deung] Conflict
- 갈색 [gal-saek] Brown
- 갈아타는 곳 [ga-ra-ta-neun-got] Transfer gate
- 갈증 [gal-jeung] Thirst

- 감 [gam] Perssimon
- 감기 [gam-gi] Cold
- 감기약 [gam-gi-yak] Cold medicine
- 감사 [gam-sa] Thanks
- 감상 [gam-sang] Appreciation
- 감자 [gam-ja] Potato
- 감정 [gam-jeong] Feeling / Emotion
- 감추다 [gam-chu-da] Hide / Conceal
- 갑부 [gap-bu] Rich man
- 강 [gang] River
- 강단 [gang-dan] Platform
- 강사 [gang-sa] Lecturer
- 강조 [gang-jo] Stress / Emphasis
- 강철 [gang-cheol] Steel
- 개 [gae] Dog
- 개괄 [gae-gwal] Summary
- 개구리 [gae-gu-ri] Frog
- 개미 [gae-mi] Ant
- 개선 [gae-seon] Triumphal return
- 개울 [gae-ul] Stream
- 개인 [gae-in] Individual / Personnel
- 개장 [gae-jang] Opening
- 개조 [gae-jo] Remodeling
- 개척 [gae-cheok] Exclamation
- 거리 [geo-ri] Street / Distance
- 거미 [geo-mi] Spider
- 거스름돈 [geo-seu-reum-don] Change
- 건강 [geon-gang] Health
- 건전지 [geon-jeon-ji] Battery

● 게 [ge] **Crab**

● 경험 [gyeong-heom] **Experience**

● 계산 [gye-san] **Check / Calculate**

● 계산서 [gye-san-seo] **Bill**

● 계약 [gye-yak] **Agreement**

● 계획 [gye-hoek] **Plan / Project**

● 고객 [go-gaek] **Customer / Client**

● 고궁 [go-gung] **Ancient palace**

● 고기 [go-gi] **Meat / Beef / Fish**

● 고독 [go-dok] **Loneliness**

● 고등학교 [go-deung-hak-gyo] **High school**

● 고민 [go-min] **Agony / Anguish**

● 고백 [go-baek] **Confession / Admission**

● 고생 [go-saeng] **Hardships / Difficulties**

● 고속도로 [go-sok-do-ro] **Highway / Expressway**

● 고양이 [go-yang-i] **Cat / Kitten**

● 고장 [go-jang] **Broke down / Trouble**

● 곡식 [gok-sik] **Cereal / Grain**

● 공간 [gong-gan] **Space / Room**

● 공기 [gong-gi] **Air**

● 공연 [gong-yeon] **Performance**

● 공원 [gong-won] **Park**

● 공장 [gong-jang] **Factory / Plant**

● 공주 [gong-ju] **Princess**

● 공중전화 [gong-jung-jeon-hwa] **Public phone / Pay phone**

● 공항 [gong-hang] **Airport**

● 공항세 [gon-hang-se] **Airport tax**

● 과일 [gwa-il] **Fruit**

● 관광 [gwan-gwang] **Sightseeing / Tourism**

- 관중 [gwan-jung] Audience / Spectator
- 광고 [gwang-go] Advertisement
- 교통 [gyo-tong] Transportation
- 교환 [gyo-hwan] Operator
- 교회 [gyo-hoe] Church
- 구급차 [gu-guep-cha] Ambulance
- 구두 [gu-du] Shoes
- 구명 조끼 [gu-myeong-jo-kki] Life vest
- 국가 [guk-ga] Nation / State / Country
- 국경일 [guk-gyeong-il] National holiday
- 국내선 [guk-nae-seon] Domestic service
- 국보 [guk-bo] National treasure
- 국적 [guk-jeok] Nationality
- 국제공항 [gug-je-gong-hang] International airport
- 국제선 [guk-je-seon] International service
- 국제운전면허 [guk-je-un-jeon-myeon-heo] International driving license
- 국제전화 [guk-je-jeon-hwa] International call / Oversea's call
- 국회 [guk-hoe] National Assembly
- 귀걸이 [gwi-geo-ri] Earrings
- 그림자 [geu-rim-ja] Shadow
- 극장 [geuk-jang] Theater
- 기념 [gi-nyeom] Memory of / Token of
- 기념품점 [gi-nyeom-pum-jeom] Souvenir shop
- 기능 [gi-neung] Function
- 기다리다 [gi-da-ri-da] Wait for
- 기본 [gi-bon] Foundation / Basis
- 기술 [gi-sul] Technique / Art
- 기억 [gi-eok] Memory / Remembrance
- 기자 [gi-ja] Journalist / Reporter

- 기준 [gi-jun] Standard / Basis
- 기차 [gi-cha] Train
- 기호 [gi-ho] ❶ Liking ❷ Taste
- 기후 [gi-hu] Climate
- 길 [gil] Way
- 깃 [git] Collar
- 꼭대기 [ggok-dae-gi] Top / Summit
- 꿈 [kkum] Dream
- 끝 [kkeut] End

ㄴ

- 나 [na] I
- 나라 [na-ra] Country / Land
- 나무 [na-mu] Tree
- 나비 [na-bi] Butterfly
- 나이 [na-i] Age
- 나중에 [na-jung-e] Later
- 낙엽 [nak-yeop] Fallen leaves
- 낙타 [nak-ta] Camel
- 난방 [nan-bang] Heating
- 날 [nal] Day
- 날개 [nal-gae] Wing
- 날다 [nal-da] Fly
- 날씨 [nal-ssi] Weather
- 낡은 [nal-geun] Old / Out-dated
- 남자 [nam-ja] Man
- 남쪽 [nam-jjok] South
- 남편 [nam-pyeon] Husband

- 낫다 [nat-da] Recover / Get well
- 낭비 [nang-bi] Waste
- 내과의사 [nae-gwa-ui-sa] Physician
- 내용 [nae-yong] Contents / Substance
- 내의 [nae-ui] Underwear
- 내일 [nae-il] Tomorrow
- 냉동식품 [naeng-dong-sik-pum] Frozen food
- 냉방 [naeng-bang] Air conditioning
- 냉장고 [naeng-jang-go] Refrigerator
- 너 [neo] You
- 노동 [no-dong] Labor
- 노랑 [no-rang] Yellow
- 노래 [no-rae] Song
- 노력 [no-ryeok] Endeavor / Effort
- 노인 [no-in] Old man
- 녹차 [nok-cha] Green tea
- 논문 [non-mun] Article / Treatise / Thesis
- 농촌 [nong-chon] Farm Village
- 높이 [no-pi] Height
- 누이 [nu-i] Sister
- 눈 [nun] ❶ Eye ❷ Snow
- 눈물 [nun-mul] Tear
- 느낌 [neu-kkim] Impression / Feeling
- 늙은이 [neul-geun-i] Old man
- 늦다 [neut-da] Be late

ㄷ

- 다갈색 [da-gal-saek] Brown

- 다람쥐 [da-ram-jwi] Squirrel / Chipmunk
- 다리 [da-ri] Bridge / Leg
- 다리미 [da-ri-mi] Iron
- 다섯 [da-seot] Five
- 단풍 [dan-pung] Maple
- 달 [dal] the Moon
- 달걀 [dal-gyal] Egg
- 달력 [dal-ryeok] Calendar
- 닭 [dak] Hen
- 닭고기 [dak-go-gi] Chicken
- 담배 [dam-bae] Cigarette / Tobacco
- 담요 [dam-nyo] Blanket
- 당근 [dang-geun] Carrot
- 당신 [dang-sin] You
- 대기시간 [dae-gi-si-gan] Waiting time
- 대나무 [dae-na-mu] Bamboo
- 대로 [dae-ro] Avenue
- 대머리 [dae-meo-ri] Bold-headed man
- 대양 [dae-yang] Ocean
- 대지 [dae-ji] Earth
- 대학 [dae-hak] University / College
- 대한민국 [dae-han-min-guk] The Republic of Korea
- 대합실 [dae-hap-sil] Waiting room
- 더러운 [deo-reo-un] Dirty
- 더운 [deo-un] Hot
- 도둑 [do-duk] Thief / Robber
- 도서관 [do-seo-gwan] Library
- 도시 [do-si] City
- 도움 [do-um] Help / Assistance

- 도전 [do-jeon] **Challenge**
- 도착 [do-chak] **Arrival**
- 독립 [dong-nip] **Independence**
- 독서 [dok-seo] **Reading**
- 독자 [dok-ja] **Reader / Subscriber**
- 돈 [don] **Money**
- 돌 [dol] **Stone**
- 돌다 [dol-da] **Turn**
- 동무 [dong-mu] **Friend / Companion**
- 동물 [dong-mul] **Animal**
- 동물원 [dong-mul-won] **Zoo**
- 동양 [dong-yang] **Orient**
- 동전 [dong-jeon] **Coin**
- 동쪽 [dong-jjok] **East**
- 동화 [dong-hwa] **Fairy Tale**
- 돼지고기 [dwae-ji-go-gi] **Pork**
- 따님 [tta-nim] **Daughter**
- 뚜껑 [ttuk-kkeong] **Cap / Lid**
- 뜻 [tteut] **Meaning / Will / Mind**

ㄹ

- 라디오 [ra-di-o] **Radio**
- 라운지 [la-un-ji] **Lounge**
- 리더 [li-der] **Leader**
- 리듬 [li-deum] **Rhythm**
- 린스 [lin-seu] **Hair conditioner / Rinse**
- 립스틱 [lip-seu-tik] **Lipstick**

- 마당 [ma-dang] **Yard / Court**
- 마스카라 [ma-seu-ka-ra] **Mascara**
- 만년필 [man-nyeon-pil] **Fountain pen**
- 만석 [man-seok] **Full seat / No seat**
- 말 [mal] **Horse**
- 맛 [mat] **Taste / Flavor**
- 매니큐어 [mae-ni-kyu-eo] **Nail enamel**
- 매력 [mae-ryeok] **Charm**
- 매미 [mae-mi] **Cicada**
- 매일 [mae-il] **Every day**
- 매장 [mae-jang] **Counter**
- 매표소 [mae-pyo-so] **Ticket office / Ticket booth**
- 맥주 [maek-ju] **Beer**
- 머물다 [meo-mul-da] **Stay**
- 멀리 [meol-ri] **Far away**
- 메뉴 [me-nyu] **Menu**
- 며느리 [myeo-neu-ri] **Daughter-in-law**
- 면세품 [myeon-se-pum] **Tax(duty)-free items**
- 명예 [myeong-ye] **Honor / Glory**
- 모래 [mo-rae] **Sand**
- 모습 [mo-seup] **Appearance**
- 모퉁이 [mo-tung-i] **Corner**
- 모험 [mo-heom] **Adventure / Risk**
- 목걸이 [mok-geo-ri] **Necklace**
- 목적 [mok-jeok] **Purpose**
- 목적지 [mok-jeok-jji] **Destination**
- 무 [mu] **Radish**

- 무늬 [mu-ni] Pattern / Design
- 무료 [mu-ryo] Free / No charge
- 무역 [mu-yeok] Trade
- 무지개 [mu-ji-gae] Rainbow
- 문 [mun] Door / Gate
- 문명 [mun-myeong] Civilization
- 문학 [mun-hak] Literature
- 물건 [mul-geon] Thing / Goods / Article
- 뮤지컬 [myu-ji-keol] Musical
- 미소 [mi-so] Smile
- 미인 [mi-in] Beautiful Woman
- 미혼의 [mi-hon-ui] Unmarried / Single
- 민요 [min-yo] Folk song

ㅂ

- 바 [ba] Bar
- 바늘 [ba-neul] Pin / Needle
- 바다 [ba-da] Sea / Ocean
- 바닷가 [ba-dat-ga] Coast / Sea shore / Beach
- 바람 [ba-ram] Wind
- 바보 [ba-bo] Fool / Idiot / Stupid / Moron
- 바위 [ba-wi] Rock
- 바지 [ba-ji] Trousers / Pants
- 박물관 [bak-mul-gwan(bangmulgwan)] Museum
- 박사 [bak-sa] Doctor
- 반 [ban] Half
- 반대 [ban-dae] Opposition / Objection
- 반응 [ban-eung] Reaction

- 반지 [ban-ji] **Ring**
- 발가락 [bal-ga-rak] **Toe**
- 발달 [bal-dal] **Development / Growth**
- 발레 [bal-re] **Ballet**
- 발표 [bal-pyo] **Announcement**
- 밤 [bam] ❶ **Night** ❷ **Nut**
- 방학 [bang-hak] **Vacation / School break**
- 배 [bae] ❶ **Ship** ❷ **Pear** ❸ **Stomach**
- 배추 [bae-chu] **Cabbage**
- 백 [baek] **Hundred**
- 백합 [baek-hap] **Lily**
- 백화점 [baek-hwa-jeom] **Department store**
- 뱀 [baem] **Snake**
- 버릇 [beo-reut] **Habit**
- 베개 [be-gae] **Pillow**
- 병 [byeong] **Bottle**
- 보물 [bo-mul] **Treasure**
- 보험 [bo-heom] **Insurance**
- 보험회사 [bo-heom-hoe-sa] **Insurance company**
- 봉투 [bong-tu] **Envelope**
- 부부 [bu-bu] **Couple**
- 부족 [bu-jok] **Scarcity / Shortage**
- 부친 [bu-chin] **Father**
- 북쪽 [buk-jjok] **North**
- 분실 [bun-sil] **Loss**
- 브로치 [beu-ro-chi] **Broach**
- 블라우스 [beul-la-u-seu] **Blouse**
- 비 [bi] **Rain**
- 비누 [bi-nu] **Soap**

- 비밀 [bi-mil] **Secret**
- 비상구 [bi-sang-gu] **Emergency exit**
- 비자 [bi-ja] **Visa**
- 비평 [bi-pyeong] **Criticism / Comment**
- 빌리다 [bil-ri-da] **Rent**
- 빚 [bit] **Debt / Loan**

ㅅ

- 사건 [sa-geon] **Event / Incident**
- 사고 [sa-go] **Accident**
- 사랑 [sa-rang] **Love / Affection**
- 사용료 [sa-yong-nyo] **Fee**
- 사전 [sa-jeon] **Dictionary**
- 사치 [sa-chi] **Luxury / Extravagance**
- 산문 [san-mun] **Prose**
- 삼월 [sam-wol] **March**
- 상 [sang] ❶ **Prize** ❷ **Table**
- 상징 [sang-jing] **Symbol / Emblem**
- 상추 [sang-chu] **Lettuce**
- 상표 [sang-pyo] **Brand**
- 새벽 [sae-byeok] **Dawn / Daybreak**
- 샐러드 [sael-reo-deu] **Salad**
- 샐러리 [sael-reo-ri] **Celery**
- 생맥주 [saeng-maek-ju] **Draft beer**
- 생명 [saeng-myeong] **Life**
- 생산 [saeng-san] **Production**
- 생선 [saeng-seon] **Fish**
- 서류 [seo-ryu] **Document / Paper**

- 서류가방 [seo-ryu-ga-bang] **Brief case**
- 서명 [seo-myeong] **Signature / Autography**
- 석유 [seok-yu] **Petroleum**
- 선물 [seon-mul] **Gift**
- 선탠오일 [seon-taen-oil] **Suntan oil**
- 설계 [seol-gye] **Plan / Design**
- 설탕 [seol-tang] **Sugar**
- 성냥 [seong-nyang] **Match**
- 세계 [se-gye] **World**
- 세관 [se-gwan] **Customs**
- 세금 [se-geum] **Tax**
- 세무서 [se-mu-seo] **Tax office**
- 세탁 [se-tak] **Cleaning / Laundry**
- 셔츠 [syeo-cheu] **Shirt**
- 소고기 [so-go-gi] **Beef**
- 소금 [so-geum] **Salt**
- 소년 [so-nyeon] **Boy**
- 소설 [so-seol] **Novel**
- 소설가 [so-seol-ga] **Novelist**
- 소스 [sso-seu] **Sauce**
- 소포 [so-po] **Parcel**
- 손녀 [son-nyeo] **Grand daughter**
- 손자 [son-ja] **Grand son**
- 송아지고기 [song-a-ji-go-gi] **Veal**
- 쇠고기 [soe-go-gi] **Beef**
- 숄더백 [syol-deo-baek] **Shoulder bag**
- 수도 [su-do] ❶ **Capital city** ❷ **Piped water**
- 수리 [su-ri] **Repair**
- 수상 [su-sang] **Prime Minister**

● 수수료 [su-su-ryo] Commission

● 수수한 [su-su-han] Plain

● 수영장 [su-yeong-jang] Swimming pool

● 숙박시설 [suk-bak-si-seol] Accommodation

● 숙박지 [suk-bak-ji] Staying place

● 순금 [sun-geum] Pure gold / Genuine gold

● 술 [sul] Liquor

● 술집 [sul-jip] Pub / Tavern

● 쉰 [swin] ❶ Fifty ❷ Spoild food

● 스물 [seu-mul] Twenty

● 스케줄 [seu-ke-jul] Schedule

● 승무원 [seung-mu-won] Crew

● 시내 [si-nae] Downtown

● 시월 [si-wol] October

● 시인 [si-in] Poet

● 시작 [si-jak] Start

● 시청 [si-cheong] City hall

● 식당 [sik-dang] Restaurant

● 식당차 [sik-dang-cha] Dinining car

● 식량 [sik-nyang(singnyang)] Food

● 식물 [sik-mul] Plant / Vegetation

● 식물원 [sik-mul-won] Botanical garden

● 식사 [sik-sa] Meal

● 신문 [sin-mun] Newspaper

● 신사복 [sin-sa-bok] Men's clothes

● 실망 [sil-mang] Disappointment

● 십이월 [sib-i-wol] December

- 아기 [a-gi] **Baby**
- 아내 [a-nae] **Wife**
- 아들 [a-deul] **Son**
- 아버지 [a-beo-ji] **Father**
- 아우 [a-u] **Brother**
- 아저씨 [a-jeo-ssi] **Uncle**
- 아주머니 [a-ju-meo-ni] **Aunt**
- 아침 [a-chim] **Morning**
- 아침식사 [a-chim-sik-sa] **Breakfast**
- 아홉 [a-hop] **Nine**
- 아흔 [a-heun] **Ninety**
- 안개 [an-gae] **Fog**
- 안내소 [an-nae-so] **Information center**
- 안내책자 [an-nae-chaek-ja] **Brochure**
- 안전 [an-jeon] **Safety / Security**
- 안전벨트 [an-jeon-belteu] **Seat belt**
- 알 [al] **Egg**
- 암 [am] **Cancer**
- 암탉 [am-tak] **Hen**
- 애국심 [ae-guk-sim] **Patriotism**
- 애인 [ae-in] **Lover / Sweet heart**
- 야구 [ya-gu] **Baseball**
- 약국 [yak-guk] **Drugstore / Pharmacy**
- 약품 [yak-pum] **Medicine / Drugs**
- 얇은 [yal-bun] **Thin**
- 양말 [yang-mal] **Socks**
- 양복 [yang-bok] **Suit**

- 어두운 / 진한 [eo-du-un] Dark
- 어린이 [eo-rin-i] Children
- 어머니 [eo-meo-ni] Mother
- 어부 [eo-bu] Fisherman
- 어제 [eo-je] Yesterday
- 얼굴 [eol-gul] Face
- 얼음 [eol-eum] Ice
- 여권 [yeo-gwon] Passport
- 여름 [yeo-reum] Summer
- 여성 [yeo-seong] Woman / Female
- 여승무원 [yeo-seung-mu-won] Stewardess
- 여행가방 [yeo-haeng-ga-bang] Suitcase
- 여행사 [yeo-haeng-sa] Travel agent
- 여행자 [yeo-haeng-ja] Traveler
- 여행자 수표 [yeo-haeng-ja-su-pyo] Traveler's checks
- 역 [yeok] Station
- 역사 [yeok-sa] History
- 연극 [yeon-geuk] Play
- 영수증 [yeong-su-jeung] Receipt
- 영화 [yeong-hwa] Movie / Film
- 옆 [yeop] Beside/ By
- 예술 [ye-sul] Art
- 예약 [ye-yak] Reservation
- 예의 [ye-ui] Courtesy
- 예절 [ye-jeol] Etiquette
- 오 [o] Five
- 오늘의 요리 [o-neul-ui-yo-ri] Today's special
- 오른쪽 [o-reun-jjok] Right side
- 오월 [o-wol] May

- 오이 [o-i] Cucumber
- 오전 [o-jeon] Forenoon
- 오해 [o-hae] Misunderstanding
- 오후 [o-hu] Afternoon
- 올해 [ol-hae] This year
- 왕자 [wang-ja] Prince
- 외과의사 [oe-gwa-ui-sa] Surgeon
- 외교 [oe-gyo] Diplomacy
- 외국 [oe-guk] Foreign Country
- 외출 [oe-chul] Outing
- 요금 [yo-geum] Charge
- 요리 [yo-ri] Dish
- 우산 [u-san] Umbrella
- 우유 [u-yu] Milk
- 우정 [u-jeong] Friendship
- 우체국 [u-che-guk] Post office
- 우체통 [u-che-tong] Post box
- 우편 [u-pyeon] Mail
- 우편엽서 [u-pyeon-yeop-seo] Post card
- 우표 [u-pyo] Stamp
- 운동장 [un-dong-jang] Playground
- 운동화 [un-dong-hwa] Sneakers
- 운명 [un-myeong] Fate / Destiny
- 운전 [un-jeon] Operation / Driving
- 운전면허증 [un-jeon-myeon-heo-jeung] Driver's license
- 운전자 [un-jeon-ja] Driver
- 원숭이 [won-sung-i] Monkey
- 유료도로 [yu-ryo-do-ro] Toll road
- 유명한 [yu-myeong-han] Famous / Well - known

- 유월 [yu-wol] June
- 은행 [eun-haeng] Bank
- 음력 [eum-nyeok] lunar Calendar
- 음성 [eum-seong] Voice
- 음악회 [eum-ak-hoe] Concert
- 의류 [ui-ryu] Clothing
- 의사 [ui-sa] Doctor
- 이륙 [i-ryuk] Take off
- 이별 [i-byeol] Separation/Parting
- 이십 [i-sip] Twenty
- 이웃 [i-ut] Neighborhood
- 이월 [i-wol] February
- 이익 [i-ik] Profit / Benefit
- 이해 [i-hae] Understanding
- 익살 [ik-sal] Humor
- 일기 [il-gi] Diary
- 일상생활용품 [il-sang-saeng-hwal-yong-pum] Daily necessities
- 일월 [il-wol] January
- 임대계약서 [im-dae-gye-yak-seo] Rental agreement
- 입구 [ip-gu] Entrance
- 입석 [ip-seok] Standing room

ㅈ

- 자극 [ja-geuk] Impetus / Stimulation
- 자다 [ja-da] Sleep
- 자동차 [ja-dong-cha] Automobile
- 자매 [ja-mae] Sisters
- 자살 [ja-sal] Suicide

- 자유 [ja-yu] Liberty
- 자전거 [ja-jeon-geo] Bicycle
- 자주 [ja-ju] Independence
- 작가 [jak-ga] Author
- 작품 [jak-pum] Work
- 잔 [jan] Glass
- 잔돈 [jan-don] Change
- 잘못 [jal-mot] Mistake / Error / Fault
- 잡지 [jap-ji] Magazine
- 장난감 [jang-nan-gam] Toy
- 장님 [jang-nim] Blind Man
- 장마 [jang-ma] Long rain / Rainy season
- 장모 [jang-mo] Mother-in-law
- 장미 [jang-mi] Rose
- 장소 [jang-so] Place
- 재능 [jae-neung] Talent / Ability / Gift
- 재료 [jae-ryo] Material
- 재물 [jae-mul] Riches / Property / Wealthy
- 재미 [jae-mi] Fun / Interest
- 재혼 [jae-hon] Remarriage
- 쟁반 [jaeng-ban] Tray
- 저금 [jeo-geum] Saving / Deposit
- 저녁 [jeo-nyeok] Evening
- 저수지 [jeo-su-ji] Reservoir
- 저택 [jeo-taek] Residence
- 적 [jeok] Enemy
- 절망 [jeol-mang] Despair
- 절약 [jeol-yak] Economy
- 점 [jeom] Fortune-telling

- 점심식사 [jeom-sim-sik-sa] Lunch
- 접시 [jeop-ssi] Plate / Saucer/ Dish
- 조개 [jo-gae] Shellflsh
- 조국 [jo-guk] Father land
- 졸업 [jol-eop] Graduation / Commencement
- 좌석 [jwa-seok] Seat
- 죄 [joe] Sin / Crime
- 주문 [ju-mun] Order
- 주유소 [ju-yu-so] Gas station
- 주차장 [ju-cha-jang] Parking lot
- 주화 [ju-hwa] Coin
- 중국요리 [jung-guk-yo-ri] Chinese food
- 지갑(동전) [ji-gap] Purse
- 지갑(지폐) [ji-gap] Wallet
- 지구 [ji-gu] Earth / Globe
- 지도 [ji-do] Map / Atlas
- 지배인 [ji-bae-in] Manager
- 지붕 [ji-bung] Roof
- 지역번호 [ji-yeok-beon-ho] Area code
- 지옥 [ji-ok] Hell
- 지주 [ji-ju] Land Owner / Land lord
- 지폐 [ji-pye] Bill
- 지하 [ji-ha] Underground
- 지하철 [ji-ha-cheol] Subway
- 지혜 [ji-hye] Wisdom
- 직업 [jik-eop] Occupation
- 직통전화 [jik-tong-jeon-hwa] Direct Phone
- 진리 [jil-ri] Truth
- 진주 [jin-ju] Pearl

- 질서 [jil-seo] Order
- 짐수레 [jim-su-re] Cart
- 집단 [jip-dan] Group / Mass
- 짧은 [jjal-bun] Short

ㅊ

- 차 [cha] ❶ Tea ❷ Car / Vehicle
- 차고 [cha-go] Garage
- 차례 [cha-rye] Order / Turn
- 차이 [cha-i] Difference
- 차표 [cha-pyo] Ticket
- 착륙 [chak-nyuk] Landing
- 찬성 [chan-seong] Approval / Agreement
- 참고 [cham-go] Reference
- 참석 [cham-seok] Attendance
- 창구 [chang-gu] Counter
- 창문 [chang-mun] Window
- 창조 [chang-jo] Creation
- 창측 [chang-cheuk] Window side
- 찾다 [cha-da] Look for / find / seek / search for
- 채소 [chae-so] Vegetable
- 채식 [chae-sik] Vegetable diet
- 처 [cheo] Wife
- 처녀 [cheo-nyeo] Virgin / Lady
- 처방전 [cheo-bang-jeon] Prescription
- 천둥 [cheon-dung] Thunder
- 천주교 [cheon-ju-gyo] Roman Catholic
- 천천히 [cheon-cheon-hi] Slowly

- 철도 [cheol-do] Railroad / Railway
- 철학 [cheol-hak] Philosophy
- 청년 [cheong-nyeon] Youth / Young man
- 청바지 [cheong-ba-ji] Blue Jeans
- 청소 [cheong-so] Cleaning
- 청중 [cheong-jung] Audience
- 체온 [che-on] Temperature
- 초 [cho] ❶ Second ❷ Vinegar ❸ Candle
- 초저녁 [cho-jeo-nyeok] Early Evening
- 촛불 [chot-bul] Candle-light
- 총장 [chong-jang] President
- 최선 [choe-seon] Best
- 최초의 [choe-cho-ui] First / Original
- 최후의 [choe-hu-ui] Last / Final
- 추억 [chu-eok] Remembrance / Memory
- 추운 [chu-un] Cold
- 추천 [chu-cheon] Recommendation
- 축제 [chuk-je] Festival / Carnival
- 출구 [chul-gu] Exit
- 출국 [chul-guk] Departure
- 출발 [chul-bal] Start
- 출생 [chul-saeng] Birth
- 출입금지 [chul-ip-geum-ji] Off limiits
- 취미 [chwi-mi] Taste / Hobby
- 치과의사 [chi-gwa-ui-sa] Dentist
- 치료 [chi-ryo] Treatment
- 치마 [chi-ma] Skirt
- 치수 [chi-su] Measurement
- 친절 [chin-jeol] Kindness

- 친척 [chin-cheok] **Relatives**
- 칠면조 [chil-myeon-jo] **Turkey**
- 칠월 [chil-wol] **July**
- 침대 [chim-dae] **Bed**
- 침묵 [chim-muk] **Silence**

ㅋ

- 카운터 [ka-un-teo] **Counter**
- 칵테일 [kak-teil] **Cocktail**
- 칼 [kal] **Knife / Sword**
- 캔 [kaen] **Can**
- 커피 [keo-pi] **Coffee**
- 코 [ko] **Nose**
- 코끼리 [ko-kki-ri] **Elephant**
- 코코넛 [ko-ko-neot] **Coconut**
- 콩 [kong] **Bean**
- 큰 [keun] **Big / Large / Huge**

ㅌ

- 타다 [ta-da] **Get on / On board**
- 탈출 [tal-chul] **Escape**
- 탐험 [tam-heom] **Exploration / Expedition**
- 탑승구 [tap-seung-gu] **Boarding gate**
- 탑승권 [tap-seung-kwon] **Boarding pass**
- 탑승시각 [tap-seung-si-gan] **Boarding time**
- 태양 [tae-yang] **the Sun**
- 태평양 [tae-pyeong-yang] **the Pacific Ocean**

● 태풍 [tae-pung] **Typoon**

● 택시 [taek-si] **Taxi**

● 택시기사 [taek-si-gi-sa] **Taxi driver**

● 택시승차장 [taek-si-seung-cha-jang] **Taxi zone / Taxi standing**

● 택시요금 [taek-si-yo-geum] **Taxi fare**

● 토끼 [to-kki] **Rabbit / Hare**

● 토마토 [to-ma-to] **Tomato**

● 토요일 [to-yo-il] **Saturday**

● 통로석 [tong-no-seok] **Aisle seat**

● 투표 [tu-pyo] **Vote**

● 트렁크 [teu-leong-keu] **Trunk**

● 팁 [tip] **Tip**

ㅍ

● 파도 [pa-do] **Waves / Surges**

● 파랑 [pa-rang] **Blue**

● 파리 [pa-ri] **Fly**

● 파산 [pa-san] **Bankruptcy**

● 파손 [pa-son] **Damage**

● 펑크 [peong-keu] **Puncture / Flat tire**

● 포도 [po-do] **Grape**

● 포도주 [po-do-ju] **Wine**

● 포옹 [po-ong] **Embrace**

● 포장하다 [po-jang-ha-da] **Wrap**

● 포크 [po-keu] **Fork**

● 폭탄 [pok-tan] **Bomb**

● 표 [pyo] **Ticket**

● 표시 [pyo-si] **Landmark / Sign**

- 표현 [pyo-hyeon] Expression
- 플랫폼 [plaet-pom] Platform
- 피 [pi] Blood
- 피부 [pi-bu] Skin
- 필수품 [pil-su-pum] Necessities
- 필요 [piryo] Need
- 필요한 [piryo-han] Necessary

ㅎ

- 하늘 [ha-neul] Sky
- 하루 [ha-ru] One day
- 하인 [ha-in] Servant
- 할머니 [hal-meo-ni] Grandma
- 할아버지 [hara-beo-ji] Grandpa
- 할인 [hal-in(harin)] Discount / Reduction
- 할인하다 [hal-in-hada(harin-hada)] Discount
- 합창 [hap-chang] Chorus / Choir
- 항공권 [hang-gong-kwon] Passenger ticket
- 항공사 [hang-gong-sa] Airline agent
- 항공편 [hang-gong-pyeon] Airmail
- 해 [hae] ❶ Sun ❷ Year
- 해군 [hae-gun] Navy
- 해바라기 [hae-ba-ra-gi] Sunflower
- 해변 [hae-byeon] Beach / Ocean / Sea shore
- 해외 [hae-oe] Overseas / Foreign
- 해외의 [hae-oe-ui] Overseas
- 핸드백 [haen-deu-baek] Handbag
- 행사 [haeng-sa] Event

● 행진 [haeng-jin] ❶ March ❷ Parade
● 향수 [hyang-su] ❶ Perfume ❷ Nostalgia
● 향신료 [hyang-sin-nyo] Spices
● 혁명 [hyeok-myeong(hyeongmyeong)] Revolution
● 현금 [hyeon-geum] Cash
● 호기심 [ho-gi-sim] Curiosity
● 호랑이 [ho-rang-i] Tiger
● 호수 [ho-su] Lake
● 호흡 [ho-heup] Breath
● 홍차 [hong-cha] Black tea
● 화장실 [hwa-jang-sil] Lavatory / Toilet / Rest room / Wash room
● 확인하다 [hwak-in-ha-da(hwaginhada)] Confirm
● 환불 [hwan-bul] Refund
● 환전 [hwan-jeon] Exchange
● 환전소 [hwan-jeon-so] Money exchange
● 환전하다 [hwan-jeon-ha-da] Make exchange
● 황금 [hwang-geum] Gold
● 황제 [hwang-je] Emperor
● 회원 [hoe-won] Member
● 효과 [hyo-gwa] Effect
● 훔친 [hum-chin] Stolen
● 휘발유 [hwi-bal-ryu] Gasoline
● 휘파람 [hwi-pa-ram] Whistle
● 휴가 [hyu-ga] Holiday / Vacation
● 휴게소 [hyu-ge-so] Lounge
● 휴지 [hyu-ji] Waste paper
● 흡연석 [heup-yeon-seok(heubyeonseok)] Smoking seat

MEMO

MEMO 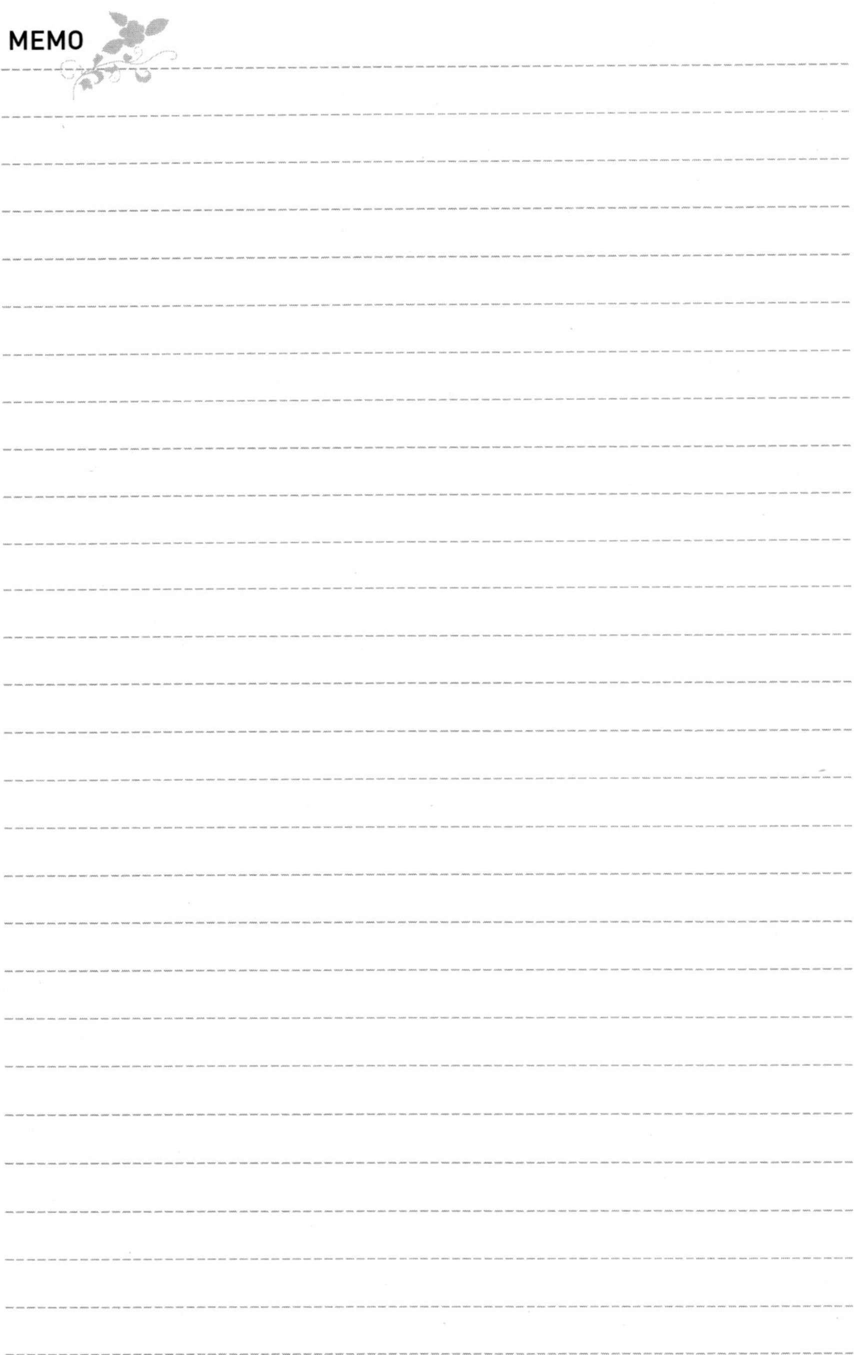